D1288943

TURF MANAGEMENT HANDBOOK

Good Turf for Lawns, Playing Fields and Parks

FIFTH EDITION

TURF MANAGEMENT HANDBOOK

Charles B. Schroeder

Head, Turf Management Department
Danville Area Community College

Howard B. Sprague

Former Head of Agronomy Department and
Chairman of the Plant Sciences Division
The Pennsylvania State University

Good Turf for Lawns, Playing Fields and Parks

Interstate Publishers, Inc.
Danville, Illinois

TURF MANAGEMENT HANDBOOK, Fifth Edition. Copyright © 1996 by Interstate Publishers, Inc. All rights reserved. Prior editions: 1970, 1976, 1982, 1994. Printed in the United States of America.

Cover Photo Credits:

Background—golf course courtesy of Terra International, Inc., Professional Products

Upper left—lawn tractor with bagger courtesy of Mollee Thomas

Upper right—Mississippi State University baseball field courtesy of Mollee Thomas

Lower left—fertilizer and spreader courtesy of Terra International, Inc., Professional Products

Lower right—chemical application courtesy of South Side Country Club, Decatur, IL

Order from
Interstate Publishers, Inc.
510 North Vermilion Street
P.O. Box 50
Danville, IL 61834
Phone: (800) 843-4774
Fax: (217) 446-9706
Email: info-ipp@IPPINC.com

Library of Congress Catalog Card No. 96-75867

ISBN 0-8134-3083-6

3 4 5 6 7 8 9 10   02 01 00 99 98

FOREWORD

Turf managers, like horticulturists, should recognize that they are dealing with natural forces, which they must understand to grow quality turf. In this respect, they are like a doctor, biochemist or scientist. The life processes are basically unchanged and the environment can be altered only locally and temporarily. There has been no change in the dependence of plants on light, water and air; the requirements of seeds for germination; and the basic processes of plant growth. The soil processes are even less visible, but are just as important to good plant growth.

The important thing to remember is that the living world is quite different from such physical matters as automobiles, computers, VCRs, and televisions. Nature is the master of all life processes, whether they involve microbes, plants, animals, or humans. The materials, equipment, and procedures developed to influence these life processes have resulted from research and testing. To the extent that these innovations are compatible with life processes in nature, they may produce satisfying results. In this book, there is an attempt to explain the natural processes involved in turf development and management, and the specific materials, equipment, and procedures that have been found to produce desirable results with a minimum of effort and expense. *Turf Management Handbook* is a practical guide to turf care for the intelligent manager and homeowner.

The role of people in modifying their environment to produce plant growth pleasing to them depends first on an understanding of the needs of the selected plant species, then on the factors of the environment that are likely to limit development of this species and the possibilities of using technology and materials to alleviate the limiting factors. Some of these factors are inherent in the plant and may be modified by choosing a different species, or by changing the management practices such as mowing, watering, admitting more light in shady areas, treatments for pests, etc. Some of the factors are inherent in the soil, and will require some diagnosis of the limitations such as acidity, aeration, nutrient supply, water relations, and humus content known to affect occupation and use of the soil by plant roots.

The authors would like to especially thank Larry Pfleiderer, Professional Products Division Manager, Terra International, Inc.; J. Michael Hart, Golf Course Superintendent, and Fritz Bateman, Assistant Superintendent, Danville Country Club; John Tonsor, Golf Course Superintendent, South Side Country Club; and Kerry G. Anderson, Rhone-Poulenc, for their assistance in obtaining current photographs of equipment, diseases, and treatment.

Charles B. Schroeder

HOW TO USE THIS BOOK

Turf Management Handbook is arranged so that the reader may go directly to the topic that is of immediate concern or to the general chapter that provides more complete information on the reasons why certain practices and treatments are recommended.

The Table of Contents lists the important subjects in the book. By noting the chapter headings, and the subtopics, one may turn directly to the section desired. For example, on weed control, not only are the management practices of control discussed, but the individual weeds are identified and control measures are detailed.

Another way of using the book is to follow in sequence the chapters on the development of the regional differences underlying turf culture, the principles of soil management, the choice of grasses, the items that should be included in standard turf treatments and the methods of dealing with difficult problems. This second method is basic to a more complete understanding of turf culture, and how to achieve desired results with the least waste of time and materials.

The two methods of using the book are complementary in nature in that counsel is given on urgent problems by the first method, and more comprehensive information is given by the second method. This second method serves as a guide to practices and treatments that are preventive in nature, since they minimize the occurrence of problems.

The Index gives the reader assistance in finding the specific page or pages dealing with an individual topic. This Index is useful in returning to an item previously noted. However, the Table of Contents is a more dependable guide to the portion of the book that gives information in sufficient depth to give the reader an understanding of the situation.

TABLE OF CONTENTS

Chapter 1

BASIC INFORMATION

INTRODUCTION

Today, the turfgrass industry is one of the fastest growing segments in the field of horticulture. In the past 50 years this country has undergone major economic and cultural changes that have had far-reaching effects on the turfgrass industry. Billions of dollars are spent annually by home-owners, to achieve high-quality, weed-free home lawns. Most of the popular athletic games in the United States are played on fields covered in natural turf. The basic principles of producing and maintaining good turf are the same for home lawns, athletic fields, parks, and similar areas. The locations and uses of turf areas often require some modifications in technique, but these adjustments are readily apparent when basic turfgrass growth principles are understood.

The objective of this book is to provide the essential information necessary for good turfgrass culture. The authors will discuss the natural laws that affect plant growth, and the management practices that apply these laws to the production of high-quality turf. The specialist in turf management performs an important role in our society. The environment in which people live, work, and play is important to their well-being. A pleasing landscape for home, work areas, or for recreation adds to the enjoyment of all those who see it. A community with a high percentage of attractive home lawns, and with ready access to healthy turf on parks and playing fields, provides an enhanced quality of living for its residents.

The initial development of areas to be turfed usually involves extensive reshaping of the natural terrain, and almost always results in land areas with a high percentage of infertile soil materials at the surface. The initial planting of grass all too often has been made without adequate soil improvement, and with temporary types of grasses unlikely to produce durable turf. Moreover, many such areas have never received adequate maintenance since the initial planting.

If the present condition of turf is unsatisfactory, there is still reason

1

to believe that the adoption of sound turf management practices will greatly improve the quality of the turf. There is no single method of producing good turf. Instead, there are many procedures that may be used by the manager that should yield results if they are not in conflict with the basic principles of grass culture, soil management, and pest control.

In the aggregate, lawns and similar turf are very important to the American public as well as to the individual homeowner. This is fortunate, since there would not otherwise have been enough research conducted on principles of turf care to establish the principles needed to guide turf managers. The research on control of insect pests, diseases, and weeds has been highly productive. The basic research on soils, fertilizers, pest control, and the breeding of improved grasses has been conducted by the agricultural experiment stations of the individual states and the United States Department of Agriculture. Stimulated by the market demand for their products, chemical companies have developed effective insecticides, fungicides, and herbicides. Equipment manufactures have also designed better sprinklers, mowers, and other turf-maintenance equipment. The great volume and diversity of grass strains, fertilizers, pesticides and equipment now available are baffling to the turf manager without an understanding of the principles of turf culture.

The total area occupied by turfgrasses on lawns, estates, parks, golf courses, playing fields, and public grounds is huge by any method of estimation. There are over 50,000,000 home lawns and more than 14,000 golf courses in this country. The turfgrass industry is big business.

It is not possible to adequately measure the role played by turfgrass in better living for people in terms of pleasure, recreation, and beauty. Neverless, turf management specialists who are responsible for the management of such turfed areas are important to better living, and they need all the knowledge and materials available from science, efficient labor-saving equipment, and access to the latest improvements in grasses and plant protection measures. Thousands of turf maintenance experts are needed each year to manage these resources.

In a huge country such as the United States, there are great differences from region to region—in climate, soil conditions, adapted grass cultivars, and turf pests. It is helpful to understand how differences in the major ecological regions will effect turfgrass culture.

TURFGRASS REGIONS IN THE UNITED STATES

- **Cool Humid Region** is suited to cool-season grasses such as bluegrass,

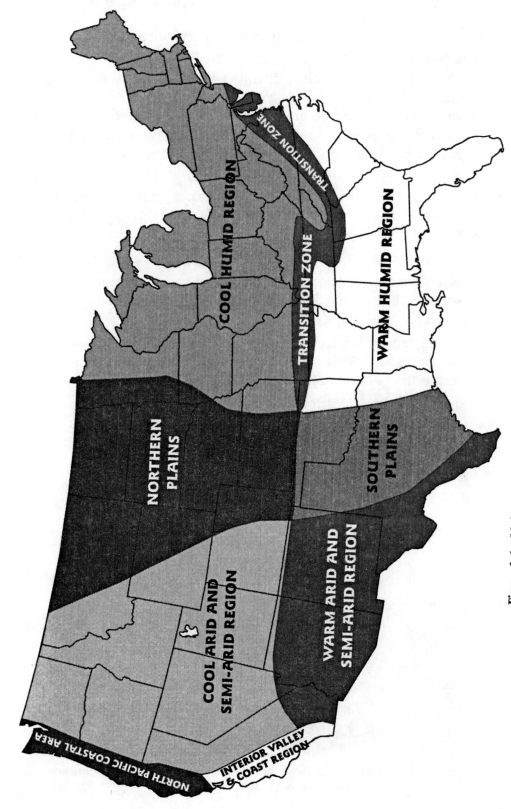

Figure 1-1. Major turfgrass zones in the continental United States.

fescue and bent grasses. Soils are generally acid, and often low in fertility. Irrigation is often needed to supplement natural rainfall.

   a. Transition Zone is a difficult zone where either cool-season or warm-season grasses may be grown. The summers are too hot for good growth of cool-season grasses, and the winters are too long and cold for desired growth of warm-season grasses. Supplemental irrigation must be used carefully to favor the type of grass desired. Soils are generally acid and low in native fertility.

- **Warm Humid Region** is suited to warm-season grasses such as Bermuda grass and St. Augustine grass. Soils are generally strongly acidic and may be relatively infertile. Irrigation may be needed to supplement rainfall.

- **Plains Region** is divided into two sub-groups.

   a. **Northern Plains Region** is suited to cool-season grasses, but artificial watering is essential for good lawns. Soils are not naturally acid.

   b. **Southern Plains Region** is suited to warm-season grasses. Irrigation, to supplement uncertain rainfall, is indispensable to the development of strong turf. Soils are not naturally acid, but are less likely to be fertile than Northern Plains soils.

- **Arid and Semi-arid Regions**

   a. **Cool Arid and Semi-arid Regions** are suited to cool-season grasses,

Figure 1-2. Well kept turf is important to the overall beauty of the landscape. (Courtesy, Danville Area Community College)

but irrigation must be provided throughout the growing season. Soils are not acid, and are generally well supplied with mineral nutrients.

b. **Warm Arid and Semi-arid Regions** are suited to warm-season grasses. Irrigation is imperative throughout the growing season. Soils are not acid, but are somewhat less fertile than regions to the North.

- **California Coast and Interior Valleys** are suited to warm-season grasses, but sprinkler irrigation is imperative during the warm, dry growing season. Soils generally are not acid, and have moderate amounts of mineral nutrients.

- **North Pacific Coastal Areas** are suited to cool-season grasses. Rainfall is generally adequate except in midsummer when sprinkler irrigation is required. Soils are usually moderately acid, and have fair-to-low mineral nutrient content.

ADJUSTING TURF CULTURE TO THE REGION

Fortunately, the basic principles of plant growth are common to all regions. Although it is true that grasses have somewhat different growth requirements than most flowers and trees, the same natural growth laws apply. What is needed is an understanding of how the various grasses

Figure 1-3. A practical, dependable mower for small home lawns.

normally grow, and how to treat them in order to achieve the desired dense sod.

In nature the soil is rarely occupied with a single type of plant, but rather by a balanced mixture of different species. To the extent that people insist on solid plantings of grass, the normal balance is broken. In the humid regions of the Great Eastern portions of the nation, and in the North Pacific regions, the land was originally occupied by forests. For grass to survive and flourish, people need to maintain the artificial balance; otherwise, the land will rapidly revert to forest. The elimination of weeds in grasslands is made possible by modifying soil conditions, moisture, and nutrition and by clipping at a height that favors turfgrass rather than taller-growing weeds. The use of herbicides is also necessary to suppress the growth of weeds. Since pure stands of grass rarely occur or persist without artificial aids, it is logical that a better understanding of the environmental conditions provides a better chance of producing and maintaining good turfgrass stands.

Climate is the major factor determining the turfgrass regions as illustrated in Figure 1-1. Such factors as temperature, length of growing season, and the extremes of summer or winter will help determine grass selection for the region. People can do little to change temperatures, so they should concentrates on changing the moisture supply, nutrients, and light supply.

Figure 1-4. Turf management students examine turf plots as a part of their laboratory instruction. (Courtesy, Danville Area Community College)

Sunlight, which is a prime requirement for all plants to a greater or lesser degree, is particularly important for good grass growth. Turf shaded by trees requires a very careful compromise in management practices to permit growth of both types of plants.

Moisture conditions are more nearly under human control, to the extent that moisture shortages may be corrected by watering. Where watering is not feasible, in humid regions or in the natural grasslands of the Plains Regions, adapted species must be used. In these areas, the manager must accept a taller type of growth and a much more limited use of the turf if it is to survive.

Moisture shortages are under human control to the extent that artificial watering is feasible. However, there is no practical way of reducing rainfall when it is in excess, nor of controlling the frequency and severity of rainstorms. Good soil drainage, if not naturally provided, may be insured by providing a drainage system to cope with excess soil water. A major problem with irrigation systems is the potential for the over-watering of turfgrass and this may occur in any climatic zone.

Some locations are exposed to excessive winds; these may be protected by plantings that serve as windbreaks. More commonly, the air movement on turf areas may be so restricted by shrubs and trees that the turf becomes susceptible to diseases damage. In all situations, it is necessary to recognize

Figure 1-5. Mowing with a lawn tractor helps maintain a pleasing landscape in large areas or playing fields. (Courtesy, Mollee Thomas)

the nature of the climate and make proper adjustments in the management of turfed areas.

Soil conditions are easier to control than climatic factors. Lime may be added to correct soil acidity conditions, fertilizers applied to supplement the natural soil nutrients, and humus incorporated to improve the level of organic materials in the soil. On small areas, the texture of the soil may be corrected by incorporating sand into heavy soils or by adding clayey materials to excessively sandy soils. Since an acre of soil to a depth of six inches weighs about two million pounds, it is impractical to do much in the way of changing soil texture on an extensive scale. The structure of the soil, its internal organization into aggregates, affects air, water, and root penetration. It may be modified on most soils using suitable treatments. For example, the incorporation of organic matter through the soil profile is effective in improving soils that are too heavy and compact. This treatment promotes the formation of granules and thus improve aeration, moisture relations and root development.

In general, the successful maintenance of turf depends on choosing grasses that are suited to the light and other climatic factors and improving the soil to suit the needs of the turfgrass. Good sound management practices such as mowing, watering, fertilizing, and pest control are also necessary for healthy grass growth. The rules are simple, but they must be followed to maintain good turfgrass stands.

Chapter 2

HOW GRASSES GROW

ROOT DEVELOPMENT

The first outward evidence of germination, after the initial swelling, is the emergence of roots from the base of the embryo (see Figures 2-1 and 2-2). These roots penetrate into the soil and develop tiny projections known as "root hairs" which make intimate contact with the soil particles. These roots and root hairs immediately begin to function in the absorption of water and nutrient elements. They also serve to anchor the seed in place.

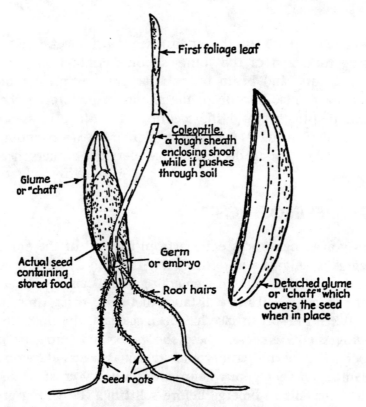

Figure 2-1. Germinating grass seed with a portion of the chaff removed to show details of development.

9

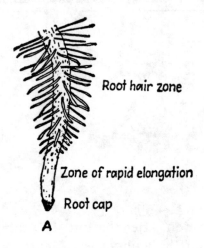

Root hair zone

Zone of rapid elongation

Root cap

A

Figure 2-2. Enlarged view of root tip (A) and greatly enlarged tip of root hair (B) showing contact with soil particles.

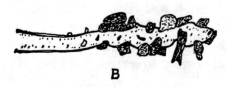

B

The reserve foods in the endosperm must meet the needs both of developing roots and of the young shoot. Germination is complete after the leaves expand and begin to manufacture new plant food supplies. If the seeds are planted too deep, the shoots cannot reach the soil surface and begin to function and the seedling dies. Since grass seeds are very small, careful planting is needed to plant seed deep enough in soil to remain moist but not so deep as to hamper shoot emergence.

SHOOT DEVELOPMENT

Shortly after new roots emerge from the end of the embryo, the new shoot begins to enlarge and push its way through the seed coat and upward to the surface of the soil. This emerging shoot has a pointed tip capable of pushing through soil for a distance of two to three times the length of the seed. When the soil surface has been reached, the tip splits, opens, and the growing shoots emerge. These shoots expand into first one leaf and then other leaves as the embryonic stem and leaves develop and unfold. When planted too deeply, or when there is a heavy crust at the soil surface, the pointed tip fails to emerge before splitting. The young growing shoot is trapped below the crust and soon dies. New seedings are often only partly successful for these reasons. Persistent sprinkling is necessary to maintain moist surface soil, without waterlogging it. However, such watering must be done with a mist-like spray to avoid development of more crusting.

NORMAL ROOTING OF TURFGRASSES

Turfgrass root systems are different in form, length of life, and manner of development from those of trees and shrubs. Grasses have fibrous root systems. The individual roots have a limited life and the root system is maintained by seasonal production of a new crop of roots. (Figure 5-2 shows a fibrous root system.)

As the young seedling develops into a mature plant, the initial roots developed directly from the seed are no longer adequate. New roots are produced from joints of the basal stem, and creeping stems if present, to meet the increased need for absorption of water and nutrients from the soil. These new roots are smaller in diameter, well branched, and supplied with tiny short-lived root hairs near the tip of each root. The development of numerous roots from nodes on grass stems in the sod produces an interlacing network of roots that completely permeate the soil. All grass plants produce this fibrous type of root system in contrast to the tap root of many other plants, characterized by a large permanent central root with many branches.

The factors known to favor a well-branched and deep root system on turfgrasses should be kept in mind when planning a turf management system. These include soil aeration and drainage, soil acidity and other toxins, adequate nutrient supply, and closeness and frequency of mowing.

TOP GROWTH OF TURFGRASSES

When the young seedlings (or shoots produced from nodes on a sprig) have developed a few leaves, new branches begin. Buds in the axils of these leaves produce their own leaves and roots. The new roots expand into the soil and absorb moisture and nutrients and these new shoots become a self-sufficient plant. These new shoots, after they mature, may in turn give rise to other shoots, thus increasing the sod density. When the initial seeding rate has been excessively heavy, there is strong competition between the individual seedlings. They all may suffer until enough die to make room for the remaining plants to use the soil and space. This accounts for the slow development seen with excessively heavy seeding rates, as compared to the stronger growth of lighter seeding rates.

CREEPING STEMS

Creeping stems are very pronounced in some species of grasses. In the case of bluegrass, these are characteristically developed below the soil surface and are called "rhizomes." In other species such as creeping bentgrass and bermudagrass, the creeping stems occur above the ground and are known as "stolons." It is these aboveground creeping stems that are used in sprigging as a means of establishing new turf. Both the underground and surface creeping stems make it possible for grasses with these traits to invade new areas. Such invasions occur most rapidly during the growing season when moisture, temperature, and nutrients are adequate. New roots develop at each joint of the creeping stems, so that the creeping stems become independent plants.

Non–sod-forming grasses do not have creeping stems and spread quite slowly by means of basal tillers or shoots on the outer portions of the parental clump. The growth of tillers is mostly upright. As each parental clump enlarges in diameter, the soil gradually becomes completely occupied with roots and tillers, thus a solid sod may be produced.

Fescue and ryegrass both have this clump type of growth habit. They are less capable of healing injuries or rapidly spreading. Some of the most troublesome weeds such as crabgrass, red sorrel, and nutgrass, spread by creeping stems.

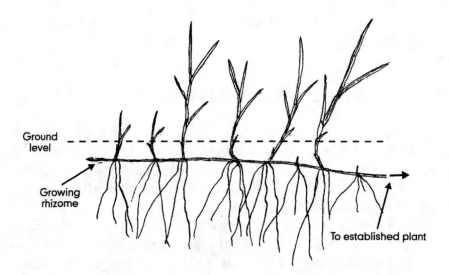

Figure 2-3. Spreading by underground creeping stems known as rhizomes or rootstocks. New aerial shoots are produced at nodes of the rhizome, each with its own root system.

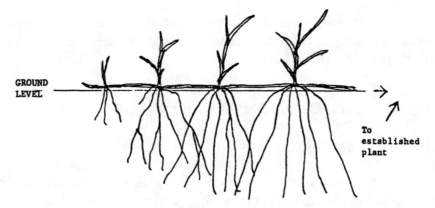

GROUND
LEVEL

To
established
plant

Figure 2-4. Spreading by above-the-ground creeping stems known as "stolons" or "runners." New shoots are produced at nodes of the stolons, each with its own root system.

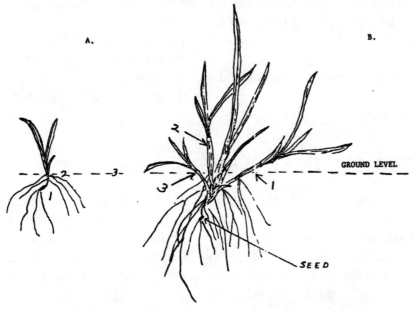

A.

B.

GROUND LEVEL

SEED

Figure 2-5. Tillering of grass seedling showing (1) seminal roots, (2) beginning of extensive fibrous root system, and (3) ground level (A). Tillering showing development of new shoots (1, 2, 3) from the initial plants, each growing its own fibrous root system (B).

LIGHT AND SOD DENSITY

All grasses tend to grow more erect in partial shade than in direct sunlight. Grass grows better during the long days of early summer than in early spring and fall when days are shorter and cooler. Some species are less sensitive to light reduction; these are termed "shade tolerant" and are useful for partially shaded areas.

EFFECT OF LIGHT INTENSITY ON TURF

Turfgrasses generally produce their best growth in full continuous sunlight. A few species are tolerant of partial shade provided they have full sunlight for part of the day. Shade-tolerant grasses should be established when natural light is the strongest, such as during the portion of the growing season when deciduous trees are without leaves. Seedlings are less shade tolerant than established sod.

It is best to lay sod where the type of tree or seasonal weather condition makes turf establishment from seed rather risky. Such sod must be composed of shade-tolerant species or it will soon weaken and die. For either seeding or sodding, a fertile soil surface should be provided. Watering partially shaded areas requires care to provide enough for healthy growth, but not too much which favors disease attacks. Avoid watering practices that keep the grass leaves moist throughout the night. Watering in shade is best done before mid-afternoon.

MOWING PRACTICES IN PARTIAL SHADE

Because grasses tend to grow more erect in partial shade than in full sunlight, raise the height of cut on grass that is growing in shaded areas to improve the quality of turf. This is particularly important on partially shaded turf. Otherwise, the leaves will be kept cut back to such an extent that food making in the leaves will not keep pace with plant respiration, and the sod will literally starve to death.

GRASSES TOLERANT OF SHORTER MOWING HEIGHTS

Most turfgrasses will respond to repeated mowing by foreshortening of stem joints and increasing the number of dwarfed shoots. Species differ in their ability to respond to height of cutting: some tolerate regular mowing at $1\frac{1}{2}$ to 2 inches, and others will tolerate mowing as short as one-half inch. Some species tolerate close mowing because of their ability to produce dwarf shoots and maintain an adequate leaf surface below the level of cutting. These special grasses are planted on golf greens and grass tennis courts.

Turf managers should remember that mowing of grass can reduce the quantity and depth of root system. Major root reduction results from close mowing. A shorter and less profuse root system means the soil moisture supply and fertility become more crucial on closely mowed turf. The ultimate effect of close mowing depends on the amount of leaf surface that the grass can maintain below the height of cut. Creeping bentgrass and the turf types of bermudagrass are examples of species that tolerate mowing at heights of one-fourth to one-eighth inch Their root systems may be only half as long on these closely cut sods as they would be if mowed at ¾ to 1½ inch height.

LEAF STRUCTURE AND FUNCTION

Each grass leaf has two principal parts: the sheath, which clasps the stem, and the blade (see Figure 3-1). The sheath not only connects the blade with the stem, but also provides strength and protects the tender new shoots that are always produced in the axil of the sheath. The leaf blades are responsible for practically all of the true food produced by the plant. The green-colored chloroplasts in leaf cells trap the sunlight. It is used for energy to combine the carbon dioxide gas entering the leaf through the pores (stomata) with water that comes from roots to produce sugars. From this beginning, starch, protein, and oils are formed that are necessary for protoplasm production. When a surplus of food is produced, it is stored in the basal stems and to some extent in roots. Whenever growth and respiration exceed food formation, the food reserves are drawn on to make up the deficit. If the deficit continues until all reserves are exhausted the plant dies of starvation.

ESSENTIALS FOR LEAF VIGOR AND GROWTH

Leaves must be continuously supplied with the essentials necessary for food manufacture. These essentials are (1) an adequate leaf area to receive energy of sunlight, (2) a continuous supply of moisture to prevent wilting, and (3) a supply of carbon dioxide gas from the air. Maintaining a suitable height of cutting insures adequate leaf area. A vigorous root system and good soil moisture provide the second requirement, and the third is met from the inexhaustible supply of carbon dioxide in the air. Besides these three prime requirements, there must be an adequate supply of all those other factors necessary for the continued health of the whole plant. The nutrient requirements and the effect of nutrient deficiencies on leaf color have been noted earlier. Of these, it is well to remember that *nitrogen* is essential for green color (chlorophyll), *phosphate* is needed for growth of new cells and tissues, and *potash* is important in translocation of manufactured foods.

SEED HEAD FORMATION

If permitted, all grasses will produce flowers and then seed heads. Species suited to cooler regions do this in late spring or early summer. The warmer zone grass species tend to produce seed heads during the last half of summer. Grassy annual weeds such as crabgrass and goosegrass behave like the warm-season perennial turfgrasses. Regular mowing will either prevent or reduce seed head formation. Annual bluegrass (*Poa annua*) is an exception. A cool-season species that grows throughout the United States, it produces seed heads in late spring and early summer though continuously mowed short.

When seed head formation is curtailed, the plant uses the accumulated food reserves for vegetative growth and this favors the production of a strong turfgrass. Infrequent mowing that permits seed head formation tends to produce an open coarse grass.

EXPLANATION OF TECHNICAL TERMS

- **Shade tolerant** means that the plants are capable of enduring reduced light conditions, such as found under trees. None of the grasses prefer shade but some are more adaptable to reduced or intermittent light than others. By contrast, there are several plants that prefer shade, such as pachysandra, ground ivy, and periwinkle.

- **Sprigging** is a general term that means the planting of cuttings, stolons, or rhizomes to establish new turf. The pieces are called sprigs.

- **Sodding** refers to any method of planting in which mature sod is used. *Spot sodding* implies the planting of pieces of sod. *Strip sodding* means the laying of sod strips at intervals, usually on steep slopes, to stabilize the soil against erosion. *Solid sodding* means that the entire ground area is covered with sod to provide an "instant" lawn. This is costly, but quite useful on important areas around new buildings, along sidewalks, on golf tees and other areas where it would be slow or difficult to establish a good turf from seed.

Chapter 3

CHARACTERISTICS OF TURFGRASSES FOR COOLER REGIONS

PRINCIPAL COOL-SEASON GRASSES

Although there are hundreds of different species of grasses, only a few are adapted to the production of turf in the cooler portions of the United States (see Figure 1-1). The turfgrasses suited to cooler regions are generally used across the United States, but in the Northern Plains and the semi-arid and arid regions irrigation is required to supplement natural rainfall. These species include bluegrasses (four species), bentgrasses (four species), fescue (two species), and ryegrasses (two species). Each species has particular characteristics, and the turf manager should match these traits with the conditions under which turf is to be grown. In seed mixtures, each species chosen should serve a useful purpose and the percentages of each kind of seed in the mixture should be adjusted to insure the desired blend of grasses. Seed size of individual species varies tremendously, from as many as 8 million seeds per pound for velvet bentgrass to as few as 250,000 seeds per pound for ryegrass.

Seed Mixtures

The price of seed mixtures is not an index of the suitability of the seed to the conditions facing the turf manager. Seed selection decisions are made according to the individual characteristics of the species and the use of the turf area. Fortunately, state and federal seed laws require that the percentage by weight of each species present must be shown on the package as well as the impurities such as dirt, trash, weed seeds, and other crop seeds.

The label must also show the percentage of live seed of each species and the date of the most recent germination test. Some grasses lose viability quickly, and thus the guaranteed germination is important since dead seed looks just like live seed.

IDENTIFYING GRASSES

The turf manager will also find it useful to be able to identify the grasses present in growing turf. The identifying characteristics are primarily those of the leaf parts and the vegetative habit of growth, with some supplemental information as to its apparent suitability for the place where it is growing. The botanist identifies grass species primarily on the characteristics of the flowers and the seed heads. The identification of turfgrasses is made by vegetative characters. It is easy to identify the genus and species of turfgrass by leaf and stem characteristics; however, the identification of an individual cultivar within a species is very difficult.

There are four principal parts of the grass leaf used in identifying grass species: (1) the *blade* (flattened part of the leaf), (2) the *sheath* (tubular portion that clasps the stem), (3) the *auricles* (claw-like appendages at the edges of the collar), and (4) the *ligule* (thin membranous tissue that extends upward from the sheath). The ligule fits tightly around the growing shoot on young leaves, thus preventing the entrance of water or dirt into the sheath. These leaf parts are illustrated in Figure 3-1. A low-power (pocket) magnifying glass is useful in examining leaf parts, particularly for species with fine leaves.

An important aid in grass identification is the shape of each young leaf in the bud before it is fully opened. In some species, such as the bluegrasses, the leaves are *folded* lengthwise in the bud and the undamaged tip of each leaf resembles the prow of a boat. In other species, such as the bentgrass, the young leaves are *rolled in the bud*

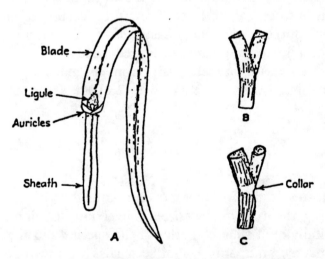

Figure 3-1. Grass leaf blade organs useful in identification of species: grass leaf (A), leaf showing folded arrangement in the bud (B), and leaf showing rolled arrangement in the bud (C).

and the undamaged leaf tips form a sharp point.

A further means of identifying turfgrasses is the presence or absence of creeping stems and the position of such stems. Grass stems growing on the soil surface are called stolons and those that grow below ground are called rhizomes. Grass species with creeping stems can make a dense sod and are called sod-forming grasses.

BLUEGRASSES

The name *bluegrass* was given to this group because of the characteristic bluish color of a field when the grass plants flower and produce seeds. When grown as turf, the only species that has any pronounced bluish-green color of the leaves is Canada bluegrass. Turf of the other species ranges from a light green (annual bluegrass) to a dark green (Kentucky bluegrass). The young leaves of all bluegrasses are *folded in the bud* and the leaf blade tip is shaped like the prow of a boat.

Kentucky bluegrass (*Poa pratensis*) (Figure 3-2) takes its name from its widespread occurrence in the fertile soils of Kentucky, but it also occurs across the northern two-thirds of the nation wherever the moisture supply is adequate. Kentucky bluegrass is not a native grass of the United States but was imported from Europe by the early settlers. It is a good species for sunny lawn areas in the temperate humid climates. It is a very aggressive grower under favorable soil conditions and can spread rapidly by underground creeping stems. Therefore, it can heal injuries and invade new areas even when the turf is in active use.

- Kentucky bluegrass produces tough, dense turfgrass when mowed at heights of $2^{1}/_{2}$ to $3^{1}/_{2}$ inches. Best growth is made in cool moist weather;

Figure 3-2. **Kentucky bluegrass and leaf parts.** (*U.S. Dept. of Agriculture Bulletin 461*)

it will go dormant in periods of heat and drought. Because of the underground creeping stems that are protected to some extent from weather extremes, the sod usually will recover from droughts or high temperatures when favorable weather returns. Kentucky bluegrass prefers fertile soil, mildly acid to mildly alkaline in reaction, with fair to good water-holding capacity. This grass is not well-adapted to shady locations and is usually weakened when cut shorter than about two inches. It is a good grass for growth in cooler periods, including very early spring and late fall, but the summer semi-dormant period becomes longer in the warmer zones farther south. Kentucky bluegrass turf is identified by a boat-shaped tipped leaf, leaves folded in the bud, and a very short membranous ligule. Kentucky bluegrass develops strong underground stems (rhizomes) and forms a dense sod.

- Rough-stalked bluegrass (*Poa trivialis*) (Figure 3-3) is a relative of Kentucky bluegrass, but differs in several important respects. It is well adapted to moderate shade unlike Kentucky bluegrass. It will thrive in sunny locations in the northern part of the cooler temperate region, but survives only in partially shaded locations in the transition region (see Figure 1-1). Turf of rough-stalked bluegrass is lighter green in color, and upon close examination it may be noted that the leaf sheaths are rough to the touch. Like most bluegrasses, it requires fertile well-drained soil. This grass generally is used only in seed mixtures for partially shaded wet areas, although it is planted in New England and the northern lake states.

  Rough-stalked bluegrass has the typical folded leaf bud and boat-shaped leaf tip of the bluegrass. The ligule is longer than in Kentucky

Figure 3-3. Rough-stalked bluegrass shoot and leaf parts.
(*U.S. Dept. of Agriculture Bulletin 461*)

bluegrass and is toothed at the tip. The leaf sheaths are rough to the touch. This species has short creeping stems, but they occur at or near the ground surface, instead of under the soil surface as in Kentucky bluegrass.

- Canada bluegrass (*Poa compressa*) (Figure 3-4) takes its name from the fact that it was first described in Canada. However, it is well adapted to all cool climates. It has limited use for turf since the turf growth is open, coarse, and relatively unattractive. Canada bluegrass has the characteristic leaf parts of other bluegrasses, but the leaf blades are short and the color is bluish-green. This grass has the merit of being tolerant of poor soils and droughty locations (steeper slopes and coarse soils with low water holding capacity). Its principal use is limited to areas with unfavorable soil conditions where soil improvement is difficult.

Figure 3-4. **Canada bluegrass shoot and leaf parts.** (*U.S. Dept. of Agriculture Bulletin 461*)

Canada bluegrass may be distinguished from other bluegrass by the typical bluish-green color of the sod, the curiously flattened stems and the comparatively open type of sod produced. The leaf characters differ from other bluegrass principally by having a shorter, wider blade.

- Annual bluegrass (*Poa annua*) (Figure 3-5) is considered a weed that is especially troublesome on the close-cut turf of golf courses. In the northern portions of the cool temperate zone, *Poa annua* has a perennial growth cycle, but in the remainder of the cool temperate zone it behaves more as a winter annual. The life cycle begins in late summer and early fall when the seeds that are present in the soil germinate and grow rapidly in the cool moist weather. It grows intermittently during the winter when the ground is not frozen and resumes active growth in early spring before any other grasses have started their growth. It produces many seed heads close to the ground beginning in late spring and continuing into the summer. The abundant seed production insures an ample supply of seed that falls on the ground. These seeds produce the next generation of plants.

Annual bluegrass has limited commercial value because of its intolerance of heat and humidity. Areas occupied by annual bluegrass are likely to become bare in the hot summer months because of the sudden death of the mature plants. Since these are important months for the golf courses, the reestablishment of a new crop of annual bluegrass in the fall period is of little consolation. This grass is more frequently regarded as a weed that hampers development of permanent turf than a desirable turfgrass.

The profuse seeding habit of annual bluegrass is responsible for its abundant survival. Annual bluegrass can invade areas where other grasses have been weakened or have died because of compact soil, unfavorable weather conditions, disease damage, or over-watering of the turf.

The natural crop of seeds germinates and becomes established in late summer and early fall when weather is most favorable. The seplants complete their life cycle by producing an abundant crop of seed before dying the following summer. This grass may be crowded out by permanent grasses under skillful management techniques that favor the desired grasses.

Figure 3-5. **Annual bluegrass shoot and leaf parts.** (*U.S. Dept. of Agriculture Bulletin 461*)

Annual bluegrass tillers profusely but does not spread to any extent by creeping stems. A thick stand of plants is necessary to produce a solid turf. The grass is shade tolerant, and it survives on compact or poorly aerated soils. Annual bluegrass will tolerate all heights of cutting, from putting green length of $1/_2$ inch to lawn lengths of $1 1/_2$ to $2 1/_2$ inches. The color of annual bluegrass turf is a brighter green than Kentucky bluegrass and the leaves tend to be much shorter and broader when both are grown under similar conditions. The plant has a tufted habit of growth with few, if any, creeping stems. The leaves resemble other bluegrass but are marked by a long ligule that does not have any teeth or notches.

BENTGRASSES

This group of four species got its odd name from the characteristic position of the basal part of each stem when plants are growing in thin stands. These stems, instead of growing upright, tend to follow the ground for a short distance and then bend upward. All of the bentgrasses have leaves that are rolled in the bud (in contrast to the folded position of bluegrass leaves) and undamaged leaf tips are always flat and pointed. Of this group of species, *redtop*, colonial bent, and velvet bent have limited turf value; however, *creeping bent* is widely used on golf courses because of its ability to produce dense turf when grown under close mowing conditions.

- Creeping bentgrass (*Agrostis palustris*), (Figures 3-6A and 3-7) is the most commonly used grass on golf putting greens and similar closely cut turf areas. As indicated by the name, this species has a strongly developed growth habit of creeping stems that root freely at the nodes. Today there are many improved commercial seed varieties available. Breeding programs at state universities and experiment stations have produced improved strains of creeping bent that are propagated by seed. Perhaps the

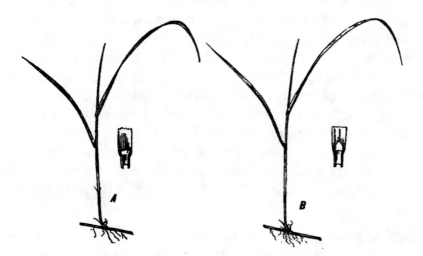

Figure 3-6. Creeping bentgrass shoot and leaf parts (A). Velvet bentgrass shoot and leaf parts (B). (*U.S. Dept. of Agriculture Bulletin 461*)

Figure 3-7. Creeping bentgrass shoot and leaf parts.

best known of these is Penncross. It is vigorous, uniform in color and texture and has considerable disease resistance. Although creeping bentgrass is well suited for turf on golf greens and other close-cut areas it is not a good lawn grass.

Under lawn conditions, the grass becomes matted within a year or two. The stems are unable to make adequate contact with the soil, and therefore become poorly rooted. When the bent declines, it leaves ugly blotches in the turf. Therefore, creeping bent should not be included in lawn seed mixtures, though the species is well suited for golf greens.

Creeping bent is not well adapted to shady conditions, but is tolerant of a wide range of soil conditions. Best growth occurs on soils of good water-holding capacity with only moderate acidity.

Creeping bentgrass may be recognized by leaves rolled in the bud, pointed leaf tips, and narrow leaf blades (less than 1/4 inch wide). Under very close mowing, the leaves become much finer but otherwise retain the same characteristics. The ligule is relatively long and pointed. Surface creeping stems are always present on lawn-length turf, and may be found in putting greens.

- Colonial bentgrass (*Agrostis tenuis*) (Figure 3-8) is not a popular species of grass for use either on golf courses or home lawns. At one time, the imported seed (known as German mixed bent) was a common source of Colonial bent seed. This mixture also contained creeping bent as well as some velvet bent, and has disappeared from the market since it is not suitable for lawns and similar turf.

Colonial bentgrass is intolerant of shade or drought and prefers sunny locations that have moderately fertile soils with good water-holding capacity. Like other bentgrasses, it does not grow at as low air and soil temperatures as bluegrass, and therefore will start growth later in spring. Colonial bent spreads very slowly by occasional short creeping stems.

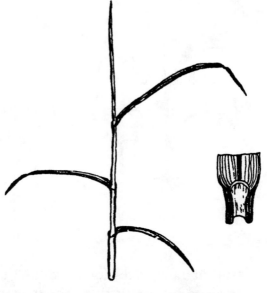

Figure 3-8. Colonial bentgrass shoot and leaf parts.

- Velvet bentgrass (*Agrostis canina*) is not a popular species because of a lack of good seed supply and its inability to do well in the Midwest clay soils. The species is mainly grown in the Canadian maritime provinces (particularly Prince Edward Island) and along some parts of the New England coast. The formerly imported German mixed bent often carried small percentages of velvet bent. It is the only member of the bentgrass group that tolerates shady conditions. It is less demanding of good soil fertility but does poorly on the clay soils of the Midwest.

    Velvet bentgrass plants are distinguished (see Figure 3-6B) by very narrow leaves (less than one-eighth inch wide) pointed at the tips, leaves rolled in the bud, and very long tissue-like ligules. There are no auricles on the collar. Under very close cutting (golf greens), the turf becomes very fine-textured, a characteristic from which it derives its name.

- Redtop (*Agrostis alba*) (Figure 3-9) is a coarse, upright growing grass, more useful for hay and pasture than for lawns and fine turf. Before 1960, redtop was included in most grass seed mixtures because of its quick germination potential. Perennial ryegrass has replaced redtop in most grass seed mixtures. The name "redtop" is derived from the color of the seed heads and has no relation to the appearance of the turf. Redtop spreads by occasional creeping stems, above and below the soil surface, when growing in hay fields and pastures. On regularly mowed

Figure 3-9.   Redtop shoot and leaf parts. (*U.S. Dept. of Agriculture Bulletin 461*)

turf, it rarely lives for more than three years because of its inability to tolerate regular cutting shorter than $1\frac{1}{2}$ inches.

FESCUES

The fescues (*Festuca* species) fall into two groups—the broadleaf group of tall fescue (*Festuca arundinacea*) and the fine fescue (*Festuca rubra*) species and subspecies. Tall fescue has long been used for low maintenance turf areas. With the recent addition of many new cultivars, many lawns are being planted with mixtures of tall fescue and bluegrass or with a monostand of tall fescue. For many years the fine fescue group has been the major shade grass for the northern cool humid part of the United States.

Fine Fescue

- The bristle-like character of the leaves makes fescue turf tough and resistant to cutting; these grasses are tolerant of drought and infertile soils and grow well in moderate shade. Only the red fescue (*Festuca rubra*) group and its subspecies (*Festuca rubra* subspecies *trichophylla*), creeping fescue (*Festuca rubra* subspecies *rubra*), spreading fescue (*Festuca rubra* subspecies *commutata*), and chewings fescue are used for home lawns or on golf courses. The improved strains of red fescue do have a limited capacity for spreading by creeping stems, and these have largely replaced the imported chewings New Zealand fescue. Because of their limited ability to heal injuries, both chewings and red fescue are better

Figure 3-10. Red fescue shoot. (*U.S. Dept. of Agriculture Bulletin 461*)

used in mixtures than alone. When the mixed turf is handled so that these fescue survive, they add wearing quality to the sod. They prefer mowing at lawn lengths of 1½ to 2½ inches. These fescue are tolerant of moderate shade, but also thrive in sunny locations. They tolerate poorer soils, but prefer soils of average to good fertility and water-holding capacity. However, since they endure moderate drought, these fescue are successfully used on terraces and other slopes where moisture supply tends to be inadequate.

The turf of red fescue is easily distinguished from other turfgrasses by the wiry, bristle-like leaves less than ¹⁄₁₆ inch wide. The ligule and collar characters are of little value in identifying these grasses. However, the individual leaves are nearly round in cross section, unlike other turfgrasses.

Tall Fescue

- Tall fescue (*Festuca arundinacea*) is a close relative of meadow fescue, but considerably larger in all respects. It is a useful grass for more extensive grassy areas that are not to be maintained as lawns. Tall fescue is a deeply rooted, strongly tufted perennial with broad, flat leaves. It tolerates both droughty and wet soils, and it grows well in sunny locations with moderate shade. It does not flourish when mowed shorter than 3 to 4 inches, and may be killed by repeated close cutting. When adequately fertilized, it makes excellent grass cover over a wide range of unfavorable soil conditions. For planting extensive areas of poor soil, where cutting at heights of 3 to 4 inches is acceptable, it may be planted alone or in mixture with perennial ryegrass. The old coarse-leafed cultivar, Kentucky 31, is seldom used today except on roadside and other very low maintenance turf areas. A new group of turf-type tall fescue cultivars, which are denser and more attractive, was introduced in the 1980s and holds great promise for the future.

RYEGRASSES

- Perennial ryegrass (*Lolium perenne*) (Figure 3-11) takes its name from a European name ("Rai" grass) and is not related to rye grain. Its quick germination and relatively cheap price have made it a popular seed to include in most home lawn grass seed mixtures today. Perennial ryegrass prefers well-drained soils of moderate to good fertility and moderate moisture supply. It is not tolerant of droughty or strongly acid soils, it suffers on waterlogged soils and it is not shade tolerant. A major problem with ryegrass is the general appearance of a lawn after mowing. Dull

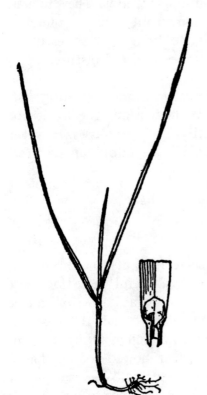

Figure 3-11. Perennial ryegrass shoot and leaf parts.
(*U.S. Dept. of Agriculture Bulletin 461*)

rotary mower blades tend to tear and shred the grass leaves, this causes the lawn to turn brown the day after mowing.

- Italian ryegrass or annual ryegrass (*Lolium multiflorum*) (Figure 3-12) resemble perennial ryegrass in appearance, adaptation, and habit of growth, but it is shorter lived and less tolerant of heat. In the Midwest it will die during the hot summer months. Very cheap grass seed mixtures will contain annual ryegrass but it is seldom used by professional turf managers today. Perennial ryegrass should be substituted for annual ryegrass in all cases.

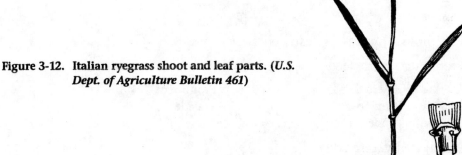

Figure 3-12. Italian ryegrass shoot and leaf parts. (*U.S. Dept. of Agriculture Bulletin 461*)

NAMED VARIETIES OF TURFGRASSES COMMERCIALLY AVAILABLE

Bluegrass

    Kentucky Bluegrass (*Poa pratensis*)

        Common non-improved varieties

Delta	Newport
Kenblue	Park
Merion	

        Improved varieties

A-20	Ben Sun
A-34	Birka
Adelphi	Bonnie Blue
America	Cheri
Aquila	Columbia
Baron	Eclipse

Emmundi   Plush
Fylking   Ram I
Georgetown   Shasta
Glade   Sydsport
Majestic   Touchdown
Mystic   Vantage
Nuggett   Victa
Parade

Rough-stalked Bluegrass (*Poa trivialis*)

Sabre

Canadian Bluegrass (*Poa compressa*)

Canon
Ruebens

Bentgrasses

Creeping Bentgrass (*Agrostis palustris*)

Propagated from seed

Emerald   Prominent
Penncross   Seaside
Penneagle

Propagated vegetatively

Cohansey (C-7)   Toranto (C-15)
Evansville   Washington (C-50)

Colonial Bentgrass (*Agrostis tenuis*)

Exeter
Highland

Velvet Bentgrass (*Agrostis canina*)

Kingston

Fescues

Fine fescues (*Festuca rubra*) and subspecies

Agram   Koket
Checker   Jamestown
Dawson   Pennlawn
Fortress   Ruby

Tall Fescue (*Festuca arundinacae*)

Coarse-leafed cultivars

Kentucky 31

Improved turf-type

Brookston	Olympic
Houndog	Rebel
Jaguar	

Ryegrasses

Perennial Ryegrass (*Lolium perenne*) improved turf-type

Birdie	Manhattan
Blazer	Manhattan II
Caravelle	NK-200
Citation	Omega
Dasher	Pennant
Derby	Pennfine
Diplomat	Regal
Fiesta	Yorktown II
Loretta	

Annual Ryegrass (*Lolium multiflorum*)

No named varieties available at present

EXPLANATION OF TECHNICAL TERMS

- **Scientific names** are always given in Latin, a custom that goes back to an early botanist named Linnaeus (about 1760). It has been continued because the scientific name for any plant is the same no matter where the plant occurs—Europe, Asia, the Americas, or Africa. Thus, scientists of all nations are aided in exchanging information. The scientific name of any plant has two parts: the genus (pronounced jé-nus) in which the first letter is capitalized and the *species* (both singular and plural is *species*). Thus, the plant we call Kentucky bluegrass is known to scientists around the world as *Poa pratensis*. The *Poa* is much like a human family name (such as Smith) and *pratensis* refer to a particular kind of *Poa*. Rough-stalked bluegrass is *Poa trivialis*, showing that it is a different member of the *Poa* genus. There may be many common names for the same plant, but only one correct botanical name for that kind of plant.

- **Common names** are useful but not very specific. Most weeds have more than one common name, and sometimes entirely different weeds or other plants are given the same common name. There are no rules for use of common names. Therefore, it is desirable to give the botanical name of a particular plant (usually in parentheses and in italic or underlined after the common name) when this is first listed in printed matter. This avoids confusion. (Note: The same system of naming disease organisms, insects, animals, and plants, using accepted Latin names, is in use by scientists and scholars around the world.)

- **Cultivar** or **variety** refers to a plant type or form within a species that has certain stabilized characteristics. These characteristics usually breed true so that use can be made of these traits. Thus, Adelphi Kentucky bluegrass always has essentially the same appearance and performance wherever it is grown. This dependable performance is very important when it involves disease resistance, density of sod, cold tolerance, general vigor, and similar traits.

- **Improved cultivars** are those that have been adequately tested and found superior in one or more desirable traits. Since it is often impossible to see the superior traits, a system has been devised for production of seed or stolons under some system of official certification so that the purchaser can be assured that the strain is true to name. Plant breeders are continuing to produce improved strains or varieties, and these are being recommended to users as their superiority is proven.

- **Rough areas** are those that are managed at heights taller than lawns. Some grassy areas may be allowed to grow wild and others may be cut occasionally at heights of 3 to 6 inches. In any event, the grass is rather tall and coarse, therefore the term "rough."

- **Sod-forming grasses** are those that make a solid cover when growing normally. The sod-forming species send out surface creeping stems (stolons) that make a comparatively dense sod (such as bentgrass) or underground creeping stems (rhizomes, on bluegrass). In both systems, the soil is completely occupied and solid cover is produced. Grasses without stolons or rhizomes make an open turf that becomes bunchy when some plants die.

- **Viability** refers to the ability of the seed to germinate and produce seedlings. Viability is expressed as percent germination under conditions of laboratory testing. It is a legal requirement that all seed offered for sale must carry a label that gives the percentage of seeds that will germinate and the date when the most recent test was made.

Chapter 4

CHARACTERISTICS OF TURFGRASSES FOR WARMER REGIONS

PRINCIPAL SPECIES

Only a few grass species are suited for turf in the warmer regions of the United States. Common bermudagrass, St. Augustinegrass, centipedegrass, carpetgrass, and zoysia. To these grasses may be added the few species that can be planted in the winter months or in special situations. These grasses grow in the warm regions across the United States, in the Southern Plains, and the semi-arid regions.

The warm-region grasses differ from each other in soil preferences, fertility requirements, shade tolerance, and the maintenance practices required for satisfactory turf. Common bermudagrass and carpetgrass may be established by seeding, but the hybrid bermudagrass, St. Augustine, centipede and zoysia grasses are propagated from sprigs, plugs, or sod. The turf manager can recognize each of these grasses by their leaf and stem characters. Many golf course superintendents over seed perennial ryegrass in the established turf during the fall season to produce a rich green putting surface during the winter months. The temporary grass literally "fades out" when warm weather recurs the following season, permitting the perennial warm-season grasses to be the dominant species.

Perennial Warm-Season Turfgrasses

• **Common bermudagrass** (*Cynodon dactylon*)—This grass grows throughout the southern humid region and the West under irrigation from Texas to the Pacific Coastal states. It is a long-lived perennial with a spreading habit of growth. The improved cultivars are propagated by sprigs, plugs, or sod and common bermudagrass by seed. It is regarded as a weed in

33

gardens and beds and in cultivated fields because of its rapid spread
when fertility and moisture are adequate. In the transition area between
the cooler and warmer regions, bermudagrass is an invader of bluegrass
turf in summer months, where it is considered undesirable since the
bermuda areas are brown in fall, winter, and early spring when bluegrass
is green.

Bermudagrass (Figure 4-1) will grow well on almost any soil that is
fertile and not too wet, but grows better on heavy soils than light sandy
soils. Common types can be established by seed sown at the beginning
of warm weather on a well-prepared seedbed, at the rate of two to four
pounds of hulled seed per acre. However, bermudagrass seed may be
planted successfully at almost any time during the warm season, if
watered. Bermudagrass responds to liberal applications of nitrogen fertilizers. The establishment of bermuda by sprigs, plugs, or sod is best
done in the late spring or summer.

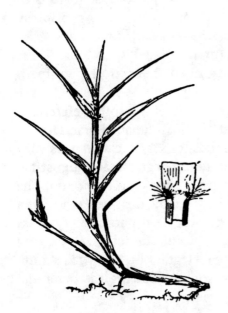

Figure 4-1. Bermudagrass shoot and leaf parts.
(*U.S. Dept. of Agriculture Bulletin*
461)

The creeping stems of bermudagrass (Figure 4-2) are tough and
white; they may occur mostly at the soil surface on heavy soils or below
the soil surface on light-textured soils. The leaves are short, flat, bluish-
green and range from 1 to 4 inches in length when uncut. At the base
of each leaf there is a fringe of white hairs; the leaf sheath is somewhat
flattened and slightly hairy.

The principal weaknesses of bermudagrass are (1) it is not shade

Figure 4-2. Bermudagrass plant. (Courtesy, U.S. Dept. of Agriculture)

tolerant, (2) it ceases growth and turns brown when average daily temperatures drop to about 45°F, (3) it has a high fertility requirement, and (4) the color is never the rich green of the improved hybrid bermudagrass. Despite these characteristics, bermudagrass has the widest regional adaptation and the greatest versatility for varying uses of all the warmer region perennial grasses. It is the most drought tolerant of the southern turfgrasses.

- **Improved bermudagrass cultivars**—These have been produced by plant breeders, principally at the Coastal Plain Experiment Station in Tifton, Georgia. These hybrids are superior in turf-producing characteristics to common bermudagrass. The hybrids were produced by crossing common bermuda with related species from Africa, and they generally produce little or no seed. These improved cultivars have leaf and stem characters similar to common bermuda, but positive identification must rely on the source and identity of the planting material. These hybrids are propagated by planting sprigs, plugs, or by sod.

The best of the turf hybrids are fine leafed, have a desirable color, generally are vigorous in growth, and are more disease resistant than common bermudagrass. Since they produce a compact and durable turf, the improved cultivars are widely used on high-quality lawns and also on golf courses and other fine turf. The sprigs used for planting should always be purchased from certified nurseries to insure positive identification of the specific hybrid. Since improved cultivars will continue to be developed, the turf manager should consult the state agricultural experiment station before purchasing bermuda plants.

- **Carpetgrass** (*Axonopus affinis*)—Carpetgrass (Figure 4-3) is the only other major turfgrass for the warmer regions that may be established readily from seed. It is much less cold tolerant than bermudagrass, and is generally restricted to the Coastal Plain area from Virginia to Texas and inland to Arkansas. It is a perennial creeping grass that makes a dense turf. The grass plants are distinguished by compressed, two-edged creeping stems that root at each joint, and by blunt leaf tips. It produces seed abundantly, when uncut, on flower stalks about 1 foot high. Seed supplies come mostly from Mississippi and Louisiana. Carpetgrass is moisture loving and is especially well adapted to sandy soils where moisture is near the surface most of the year. Although its turf is dense and its habit of growth is aggressive, it has no underground stems and is more easily controlled on tilled areas and garden beds than bermudagrass. Perhaps the greatest advantage of carpetgrass is its ability to maintain turf with comparatively little attention after establishment. It has a low fertility requirement wherever soil moisture is adequate. It has moderate shade tolerance.

- **St. Augustinegrass** (*Stenotaphrum secundatum*)—This species has earned a prominent role as the most important shade-tolerant species for turf in the southern states. However, it also grows well in sunny locations. It is a rather coarse-textured perennial that produces surface creeping stems (stolons) with long internodes. The erect branches, produced at the nodes, are short, leafy, and flat. The leaf sheaths are flat and folded and the grass blades are short and wide at the ends. Rooted sections of the stolons are planted in rows or broadcast, and covered by disking in or partially covered by topdressing. Planting may be made during the

Figure 4-3. Carpetgrass. (Courtesy, U.S. Dept. of Agriculture)

warm season but should be watered regularly whenever rainfall is not abundant.

St. Augustine (Figure 4-4) is well adapted in the Coastal Plain area from Virginia to Texas, and inland to the regions where it is no longer winter hardy. Under irrigation, it is planted in the southwestern states and California. It prefers high soil fertility and responds to liberal use of fertilizers. While it tolerates some soil acidity, it makes better growth where soils are naturally alkaline. Turf of St. Augustine has a bright green color but is relatively coarse. Unless mowed frequently at heights of about 1 inch, it may develop a mat of surface stems that become vulnerable to leaf diseases and insects.

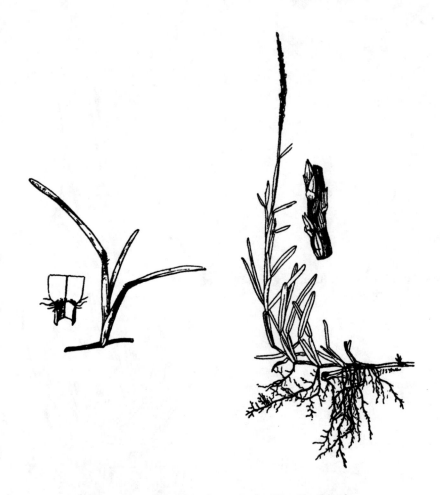

Figure 4-4. St. Augustinegrass. Left: Shoot and leaf parts.

- **Centipedegrass** (*Eremochloa oplinoides*)—Centipedegrass (Figure 4-5) probably gets its name from the shape of the seed spike that resembles a centipede insect. It produces little seed when the turf is mowed on a regular schedule. Under frequent mowing, seedstalks are not noticeable. Centipedegrass is a low-growing perennial, that spreads freely by surface creeping stems. The texture of centipedegrass turf is somewhat coarser than bermudagrass, but not as coarse as carpetgrass.

  Centipedegrass is adapted to a wide range of soils in the same geographic regions as carpetgrass and St. Augustinegrass. It will grow on clay soils as well as the poorest sandy soils if enough moisture and plant food are available to get it started. However, it responds to moderate fertilization that encourages a more rapid spread and increased density of turf. Probably the greatest usefulness of this grass is on soils that are

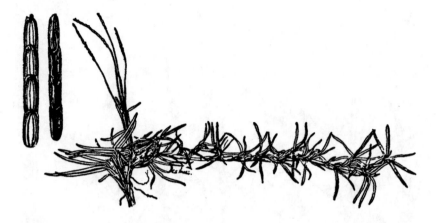

Figure 4-5. Centipedegrass stolon. (Courtesy, U.S. Dept. of Agriculture)

too low in fertility to support good turf. It is much less tolerant of drought and of cold than bermudagrass, but it is about as shade tolerant as carpetgrass.

Since commercial seed supplies of centipedegrass are not available, the grass is established by planting sprigs, leaving part of each sprig protruding above the surface. Planting may be made any time during the warm season, but watering is necessary for prompt establishment in periods when rainfall is not abundant.

- **Zoysia**— There are three principal species of zoysia grasses now grown in the United States: Japanese lawn grass (*Zoysia japonica*), Manilagrass (*Zoysia matrella*) (Figure 4-6), and Mascarenegrass (*Zoysia tenuifolia*). Japanese lawn grass, also called Korean lawngrass, is a coarse-textured perennial that makes a durable lawn. Seed is not available, and therefore this species is established by sprigs, plugs, or sod. Zoysia will grow throughout the warmer regions and will survive winter cold better than bermudagrass. However, zoysia stops all growth when average daily temperatures drop below 50°F, and turns straw colored with the first frost. In the transition zone between the cooler and warmer regions zoysia begins growth four to six weeks later than bluegrass. Therefore, it should be regarded as a southern grass. Less mowing and lower levels of maintenance are needed on zoysia lawns. While it will tolerate light shade, zoysia is not a good grass selection for use in moderate to deep shade conditions.

A limiting characteristic of zoysia is that it must be started from sprigs or spot sodding since seed is not available, and about two years

Figure 4-6. Manilagrass stolon. (*Zoysia matrella*). (Courtesy, U.S. Dept. of Agriculture)

are needed to produce a solid turf. Once established, it is very durable and persistent and endures a great amount of foot traffic without damage. Despite the presence of runners, it is slow to heal injuries of any sort. Because the plants are sensitive to cold, it is best to establish zoysia in the spring when the soil is warm to allow a full season of growth before cool weather makes it go dormant. Slow establishment also makes weed control more difficult in new plantings than with most other southern turfgrasses.

The various species and cultivars of zoysia will do well on a variety of soil types but prefer heavier-textured soils. Zoysia responds to fertility and should receive moderate amounts of fertilizer each year. Zoysia is well adapted to the higher altitudes and the northerly sections of the warmer region where carpetgrass, centipedegrass, and St. Augustinegrass are not. In those portions of the warmer regions where the bluegrass and fescue are not adapted, the turf manager has a choice of bermudagrass or of zoysia. Zoysia has a definite advantage over bermudagrass; it equals St. Augustinegrass in shade tolerance, but makes a finer-textured turf. Zoysia is somewhat more shade tolerant than centipedegrass or carpetgrass, and makes a denser and finer turf than either. It may be superior to other southern turfgrasses on heavier-textured soils that are well fertilized, but is not as well suited to low fertility and to sandy soils as carpetgrass and centipedegrass.

Special Turfgrasses for Warmer Regions

* **Shaded areas, from the latitude of Birmingham and northward to the cooler region**—Kentucky bluegrass has good shade tolerance. Although the intense summer sunlight and higher temperatures of sunny locations in this region are quite unfavorable to Kentucky bluegrass grown in full sun, it maintains good growth in partial shade, provided good soil fertility is maintained. In the cooler regions to the north, Kentucky bluegrass is not good in shaded areas and it is only in the northern portion of the warmer region that bluegrass should be relied on for growth under trees.

* **Temporary winter turf on perennial southern grasses**—The most dependable species is perennial ryegrass. Seed ryegrass in the autumn after the perennial southern grasses stop growth. Seeding should be preceded by fairly close mowing, some surface soil scarification and application of a starter fertilizer. The grass germinates promptly, despite cool weather, and will continue growth until the following spring when warmer temperatures allow renewed growth of the perennial grass. The ryegrass soon disappears under higher temperatures without damage to the permanent grass. Ryegrass requires fairly high fertilization for best results, and the turf manager should not expect the fall fertilization of the ryegrass to take the place of adequate fertilization of the warm-season grass.

* **Extensive grassed areas that do not require maintenance at lawn lengths**—The turf manager may use tall fescue Kentucky 31 in the same manner as described in the preceding chapter. Its area of adaptation is mostly north of the Coastal Plain region. Bermudagrass is adapted to the same region and may be used instead of tall fescue, or in mixture with it.

  In the Coastal Plain region, from Virginia to Texas, other grass species may be more suited to the climate and soil conditions. None of these grasses is well suited to mowing at lawn lengths of $1\frac{1}{2}$ inches or shorter, but they will survive and make a solid grass cover when mowed at heights of 3 to 4 inches.

TURFGRASS VARIETIES FOR WARMER REGIONS

The adaptation of each variety in the following lists may vary greatly from area to area in the United States.

Bermudagrass (*Cynodon dactylon*)

Golf greens

Tifdwarf
Tifgreen

Golf course fairways and home lawns

Midiron	Sunturf
Midway	Tiflawn
Ormond	Tifway II
Santa Ana	U-3

Carpetgrass (*Axonopus affinis*)

No named varieties

Centipedegrass (*Eremochloa oplinoides*)

Oklawn

St. Augustinegrass (*Stenotaphrum secundatum*)

Bitter Blue
Floratam
Floratam II

Zoysia grasses

Japanese Lawn grass (*Zoysia japonica*)

Meyer
Midwest

Zoysia Hybrid (*Zoysia japonica* X *Zoysia tenuifolia*)

Emerald

Bahiagrass (*Paspalum notatum*)

Pensacola

Chapter 5

SOIL CONDITIONS
FOR HEALTHY TURF

SOIL FOR GRASSLANDS

Grass varieties used on lawns and similar turf areas prefer soil conditions different from those that are most suitable for trees and shrubs. Some soils are naturally suited to turfgrasses, and others may be made acceptable by improvement measures. Generally the topsoil of areas that are suited to corn and small grains will produce good turf without much alteration except fertilization and watering. Particularly in the regions where grasses naturally predominate, the soil conditions are favorable for turfgrasses. The soils in these regions have adequate humus in the surface layer, are well drained, and have good water-holding capacity

By contrast with natural grassland soils, the soils of naturally forested areas (which includes nearly all of the three humid regions shown in Figure 1-1 except the Corn Belt) are suited to tree and shrub growth, but require improvement for satisfactory turf. The topsoil in areas that were originally dominated by trees is shallow, low in humus content, compact, and may be strongly acid and infertile. Where such soils have been cleared and farmed, the organic matter (humus) content is usually low as shown by light color, but the acidity and fertility have sometimes been improved.

For those who live in the Plains regions or in the sub-humid, arid and semi-arid regions, the soils are generally well suited to turfgrasses and the principal limiting factor is moisture supply. The same statements may be made for nearly all of California soils.

Thus, turfgrasses suited to a particular climatic conditions may be grown in practically every section of the United States if soils are modified to correct any inherent deficiencies. Recognition of the limiting soil conditions and adequate improvement measures will produce soils that are well suited to turfgrass and able to endure the treatment usually expected of a turf area. In considering the character of soils suited to grasses, it will be useful to consider briefly the composition of soil.

43

Figure 5-1. Soil samples being prepared for testing.
(Courtesy, Terra International, Inc.,
Professional Products)

WHAT IS SOIL?

Soil, if examined closely, will be found to contain a considerable amount of fine mineral particles, with fewer coarse particles. Normally, the particles of this mixture are organized into granules or "aggregates," and the nature of these aggregates determines the structure or organization of soil as noted by close observation. The relative percentages of the various sizes of mineral particles determine the soil structure and dictate the kinds of treatments needed.

The very fine mineral particles are so small that if a soil is shaken with water they will stay suspended; these are termed *clay* particles. The largest particles, which quickly settle out of a suspension of soil and water, are termed *sand*. Those particles that settle out more slowly are intermediate in size (although too small to be seen with the unaided eye) and are termed *silt*. Using the relative proportions of these three classes of mineral particles, soil *texture* is described as *sandy soil, sandy loam, loam, silt loam, clay loam or clay*.

TOPSOIL AND SUBSOIL

Before or during construction, grading will usually disturb the original soil; therefore, very little natural topsoil will be found at the surface. Although the spreading of topsoil following grading may have been accomplished, the layer is usually quite thin. A root system of turfgrass mowed at lawn lengths will penetrate at least 8 to 12 inches in favorable soils; therefore, it is important to improve this soil area.

If given some help, grass roots will do a remarkable job of improving poor subsoil left at the ground's surface after grading. The annual root crop penetrates the soil mass to improve its aeration and drainage. As these rootlets die, they provide food for soil microbes, and the result is an increase in humus content. Each year of grass growth should improve soil structure and make the site better suited for healthy turf.

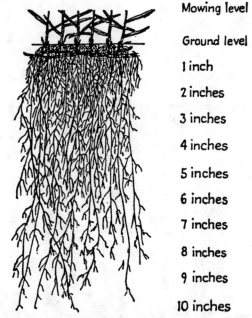

| Mowing level |
| Ground level |
| 1 inch |
| 2 inches |
| 3 inches |
| 4 inches |
| 5 inches |
| 6 inches |
| 7 inches |
| 8 inches |
| 9 inches |
| 10 inches |

Figure 5-2. Fibrous root system of grass cut at lawn length on good, deep soil. Root penetration may be as little as two inches on unfavorable soil.

The excavated material from grading, which may include material from lower depths as well as true subsoil, differs from topsoil in that it has not been subjected to the mellowing effect of plant roots. It does not have the abundance of soil microbes feeding on dead roots and underground stems, and the soil is inert. In humid regions these inert soils will supply little or no nutrients for grass roots, in sharp contrast to the supply found in fertile topsoil.

The very fine-textured colloidal matter in strong topsoil is made up of partly decomposed organic matter (roots, etc.) in intimate mixture with clay. It has the capacity of serving as a natural source of plant nutrients and as a reservoir to retain and later release nutrients and water for plant use.

Special soil conditions:

- **Alluvial soils**—Found on the flood plains of rivers and lesser watercourses and formed from sediment deposited periodically by water, these soils are often rich in organic matter (if dark colored) and nutrients but highly variable in texture.

- **Excessively sandy soils**—Although widely distributed, all sands have a low water holding capacity and are subject to wind erosion. They are generally low in nutrients, and easily leached by rainfall.

Table 5-1

Natural Soil Conditions in the Principal Turf Grass Regions

Region	Average Rainfall (in. yearly)	Natural Vegetative Cover	Natural Soil Characteristics	
			Topsoil (general conditions)	Subsoil (general conditions)
1. Cool Humid Region				
A. Cleared woodlands	30 to 50	Mostly forest	Thin, grayish-brown, acid	Yellowish or light gray, heavy textured, strongly acid
B. Corn Belt	30 to 40	Tall grasses	Dark brown, high in humus, slightly to strongly acid	Lighter brown, lower in humus, slightly to moderately acid
2. Warm Humid Region	30 to 50	Mostly forest	Thin, grayish to yellow, strongly acid	Strongly red or yellow, heavier textured, strongly acid
3. Great Plains				
A. Northern	12 to 30	Short to tall grasses	Brown to dark brown, humus stronger near surface, neutral to alkaline	Brown or lighter colored, little humus, lime nodules present
B. Southern	15 to 30	Short to tall grasses	Reddish brown (except Texas Blacklands), neutral to alkaline	Light reddish brown, heavier textured, lime nodules present
4. Semi-arid and Arid				
A. Cool, northern	3 to 12	Sparse grass and shrubs	Light grayish, alkaline	Light grayish, hardpan common, calcareous
B. Warm, southern	3 to 15	Sparse grass and shrubs	Light reddish brown, alkaline	Reddish brown, friable, highly calcareous
5. California Coast and Interior Valleys	10 to 20	Grass and shrubs	Dark reddish brown, neutral to alkaline	Reddish brown, some lime present
6. North Pacific Coastal Area	30 to 50	Mostly forest	Generally gray or grayish brown, thin, acid	Yellowish or light gray, heavier textured, strongly acid

Special soil conditions:

A. *Alluvial soils:* Found on the flood plains of rivers and lesser water courses. Formed from sediment deposited periodically by water. Often relatively rich in organic matter (if dark colored) and nutrients. Highly variable in texture.

B. *Excessively sandy soils:* Widely distributed. All sands are low in water-supplying power and subject to wind erosion. Generally low in nutrients, and easily leached by rainfall.

C. *Alkali and salty soils:* Occur locally throughout drier regions, wherever internal soil drainage is imperfect. Salty soils mostly occur on coastal plains, where sea or brackish water penetrates.

- **Alkali and salty soils**—These occur locally throughout drier regions, wherever internal soil drainage is imperfect. Salty soils usually occur on coastal plains where the sea or brackish water penetrates. Fortunately, grass roots themselves will build up this desirable fraction, even in raw excavated soils. This will take time and an understanding as to the kind of care needed to reach an acceptable condition. Not only is the expense of providing a deep layer of topsoil prohibitive, but there may not be enough topsoil available in the humid regions to supply the needs. The practical objective, therefore, is to adopt a system of grass management that will support sturdy annual growth and gradually improve soil conditions by means of the grassroot growth.

Since the nature of subsoil (parent material) and natural topsoil varies greatly from region to region, it is useful to know something about the general conditions that occur. The turf manager should develop a plan of management with these general considerations in mind. A general summary of the natural soil conditions for the various regions is presented in Table 5-1. The regions are those shown in Figure 1-1.

SOIL IMPROVEMENT

Since grass roots will penetrate soils 8 to 12 inches when mowed at lawn lengths, provide proper soil conditions to that depth when planting turfgrass. If the lawn has already been installed, then management practices need to be adjusted to compensate for poor soil conditions. When preparing a site good surface and subsurface drainage must be provide. When soils are made up of a large amount of fine particles—clay and silt—they are more likely to have poor internal drainage than loamy soils which have a larger amount of sand.

Imperfect internal drainage may result when hardened layers are created by heavy traffic on wet soils during construction or grading. Soil chiseling, during soil preparation for planting, can correct these artificial hard pan conditions. Where compacted soils are present on planted areas, power-driven aerating machines that remove small soil cores to a depth of about 6 inches are effective and moderate in cost. Where foot traffic is likely to be heavy, irrespective of rain or soil moisture, it may be necessary to seek the help of a drainage specialist who can provide tile drainage. The incorporation of lime and some form of organic matter (peat or humus) throughout the upper two to four inches during seedbed preparation is often quite successful in producing the open structure needed by grass roots.

Figure 5-3. Underground sprinklers are being used more frequently in home
lawns. They require periodic maintenance and must be
winterized in northern climates. (Courtesy, John Tonsor)

SOIL TEXTURE

Fortunately, grasses will grow on a wide range of soil textures ranging
from quite sandy through loamy to heavy loams and clays. Sandy soils can
support good turf if greater attention is given to sustained water supply
and balanced fertilization. Loam type soils provide a natural support for
the growth of turfgrass. However, sandier soils are less likely to develop
an undesirable compacted structure under heavy traffic in wet periods (on
paths, etc.), and may be preferable. It is not often that the texture of the
soil material will be a limiting factor in making and keeping good turf.
Instead of importing soil of an ideal texture, it is more practical to improve
the soil material already there. For new planting, spread an inch of mellow
topsoil at the surface, as an aid in germination and establishment of new
seeding.

SOIL STRUCTURE

Soils may differ in natural structure, but in all soils, once grass has
been established, the roots tend to improve the granular soil structure.
Good water-holding capacity combined with a very efficient system of

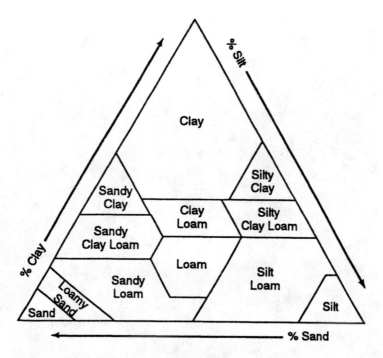

Figure 5-4. Soil texture triangle.

aerating the soil will provide the grass roots with the necessary oxygen. Soils that are strongly acid are easily puddled; the granules break down and compaction occurs. Granulation develops from root action, periodic freezing and thawing in the cooler soil regions, and by successive soil wetting and drying. The grass roots improve the soil structure to the depth that roots penetrate because the old roots die yearly, decompose, and are added to the supply of organic matter in the soil. This yearly addition of organic matter is very beneficial since the humus acts as a soil-binding agent which makes for desirable structure. Conditions that produce poor soil structure are continuing tramping of turf when the soil is wet, heavy rolling of wet soil and other compacting activities.

Grasses produce a new crop of roots each year, and normally the old roots decompose and are added to the humus content of the soil. This is a desirable process; attention should be given to promoting root growth and also to normal root decomposition. Excessive soil acidity, limited nitrogen supply, or poor internal soil drainage may produce an undue accumulation of dead and undecomposed roots. With proper soil drainage and aeration, correction of any soil acidity that may be present, and adequate fertilization the soil organic matter added by grass roots is beneficial.

Figure 5-5. Football makes heavy demands on turf in all kinds of weather.
Fields should have specially designed soil conditions to
endure such traffic. Here a football field is being renovated
by aerification during the off-season. (Courtesy, The
Pennsylvania State University)

SOIL AERATION

Grasses as a group are very dependent upon good aeration of the soil.
Roots do not penetrate poorly aerated soil layers. Soils that are light (sandy)
in texture have better aeration than soils that are heavy in texture. Moreover,
soils that have the desirable granular structure have a better aeration system
than soils that have lost structure through improper management. The
presence of liberal quantities of organic matter will improve soil structure
and aeration. Any treatment that reduces the coarse granulation of soils,
such as rolling and tramping when soil is soggy and excessive watering,
decreases the amount of air that may enter the soil. Since grass roots are
highly dependent on a continuing supply of soil air, soil treatments—either

Figure 5-6.   Using a slicer/seeder for overseeding thin turf. (Courtesy, Danville Area Community College)

at planting time or on established turf—should provide the optimum aeration.

EXCESSIVE AERATION OF SANDY SOILS

Very sandy soils are usually over-aerated and deficient in moisture and nutrient-supplying power. When heavy-textured soil is available, a thin layer of an inch or more spread on top of the sand is a highly effective means of preventing over aeration. It will also improve water retention by reducing evaporation. Fortunately, grass roots tend to grow much deeper on sandy soils, if the surface can be stabilized. When heavy-textured soil is not available, the thorough incorporation of peat or humus (intimate mixing is essential) will improve the water and nutrient relationships of very sandy soils. Merely spreading organic amendments on top of sandy soils is of dubious value; it is not likely to produce results worthy of the cost.

WARM AND COLD SOILS

In cool climates, some soil types allow early, active grass growth in the spring. Such soils have a desirable structure, are well aerated, and stimulate active growth whenever adequate nitrogen is available. They are

Figure 5-7. **Water aerification of a golf course green during the growing season to correct impervious soil structure caused by heavy use. (Courtesy, Mollee Thomas)**

said to be "warm" soils, in contrast to soils that are "cold" because of poor aeration. Sandy soils are usually considered warm compared to clay soils. They have a high water content and warm up slower than sandy soils containing less water. Sandy soils allow air to move in and out more rapidly than clay soils. It is not as important, however, to provide a warm soil as it is to provide a desirable structure, sufficient soil organic matter, and adequate aeration. The growing season for turf can be extended by choosing adapted grasses and cool-season feeding, even on a cold soil.

CHEMICAL STATUS OF SOIL

In the preceding sections, soil has been considered from a physical standpoint as a supplier of air, water, and warmth. In addition, soil must also be evaluated as the place where plants obtain the necessary nutrients for good plant growth. Soil must supply plants with the following nutrients in a usable form: *nitrogen, phosphorus, potassium, calcium, magnesium, sulfur* and the other nutrients in minute (trace) amount. All of the nutrients absorbed by roots must be dissolved in water. The nutrient quantities usually present in soil water at any time are exceedingly low. This supply is replenished regularly from several sources. One source is the mineral fragments that make up the body of the soil—the sand, silt, and clay. Clay and silt are much more important to nutrient supply than sand. Sand may be regarded as the chemically inert part of the soil, which adds little to the soil solution, however, desert sands are richer than beach or river sands. The clay fraction, on the other hand, is very important and releases most of the plant nutrients supplied by the mineral portion of the soil. Clay particles make up most of the mineral colloids of the soil. They will absorb such substances as calcium and magnesium provided by added limestone, potassium from potash-bearing fertilizers, and ammonia from fertilizers carrying nitrogen in the ammonia form.

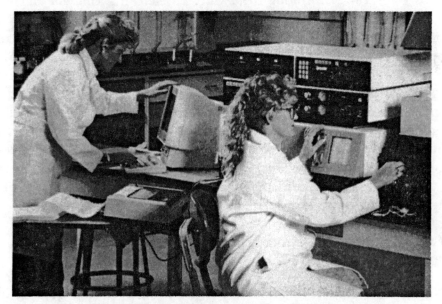

Figure 5-8. Testing of soil samples in a laboratory. (Courtesy, Terra International, Inc., Professional Products)

Another important soil ingredient is organic matter that combines with the same nutrient elements as clay. Besides these functions of soil organic matter, remember that all organic matter is in a process of decomposition. Under some conditions decay occurs rapidly, under others it is slow. When decay does occur, there is a release of plant nutrients. The more complex compounds in the organic matter are converted into simplified forms containing the nutrients that may then be absorbed by plant roots and used for growth. Thus, in a soil well supplied with organic matter and well aerated, the organic matter, through its continuing decomposition, provides a steady supply of plant nutrients. These nutrients should keep the grass growing as long as other conditions are favorable.

NUTRIENTS FROM SOIL

As noted in the previous section, grass plants (like other plants) require thirteen elements from the soil in substantial amounts if growth is to be healthy and normal. Air and water supply plants with three other necessary elements, *hydrogen, oxygen,* and *carbon.* The thirteen mineral elements may be present naturally in the soil in sufficient amounts, if not, they must be supplied by fertilizers. Among these thirteen elements, *calcium* and *magnesium* are usually present to some extent, but in acid soils the supply is so low that lime must be added for satisfactory grass growth. These elements are steadily lost from soil by the leaching action of water, by removal of plant parts containing these elements, and by the action of certain acid-producing fertilizers. *Phosphorus* and *sulfur* are necessary for plant growth. *Potassium,* commonly termed "potash," is also present in the soil, frequently in considerable amounts. Since most potash-containing soil minerals have very low availability, it is usually necessary to supply potash fertilizers to insure an adequate supply. *Iron* is an essential element, but it is rarely, if ever, needed on soils because of abundant supplies naturally present. On strongly acid soils, the excess soluble iron may become toxic.

Nitrogen

Nitrogen is the most important of all elements needed for grass growth, and it must be supplied through the soil. It is absorbed by plants in one of two forms, either as nitrates or as ammonia. Plants take up nitrates more readily on acid soils, but use ammonia without difficulty if the soil is neutral or alkaline. Both the nitrate and ammonia forms of nitrogen are produced by the decomposition of organic matter and by natural organic fertilizers. Commercial fertilizers often supply nitrogen in both forms.

Balance Between Nutrients

Good balance between nutrient elements is important. For satisfactory growth, none of the elements should be deficient, and the supply should be in proportion to the amounts required by plants. Plants need large amounts of nitrogen but smaller amounts of phosphorus and potassium.

Plants use intermediate amounts of calcium, magnesium, and sulfur. The trace elements are required in very small amounts. It is customary and practical to supplement the capacity of the soil to supply nutrients with applications of fertilizer. However, it is easy to over apply lime and fertilizer if no attention is paid to the need for balance between nutrients. The goal in the improvement of soil for grasses is to have a balanced supply of the various nutrient elements to achieve a status similar to that of a fertile grassland soil. Soil testing is one method of determining the capacity of the soil for supplying essential nutrient elements. This permits identification of the deficiencies so that they may be corrected by an appropriate kind of fertilizer or by using lime or other amendments. Grasses thrive on fertile soil; also, the more intensive the use, the greater the need for high fertility. However, this state of high fertility requires intelligent use of materials to achieve the balance between nutrients that promotes healthy growth.

Figure 5-9.　Spreader used to apply fertilizer on large turf areas. (Courtesy, Danville Country Club)

THE LIVING FRACTION OF THE SOIL

Besides the physical and chemical components of the soil, there is a third highly essential fraction—*the living fraction*. This is composed of plant roots, soil-inhabiting insects and worms, and the myriads of microbes too small for the eye to see. The microbes, in particular, are responsible for most of the transformations of dead roots into soil humus, with the attendant release of nutrients for plants. Bacteria should be present in great numbers and variety—10 to 50 million per teaspoonful of soil—as well as many molds and similar organisms of microscopic size. The animal forms are abundant, including various kinds of amoebae and other protozoa.

Earthworms also inhabit normal soil and are an important part of its life. The important point to remember is that a healthy, normal soil is teeming with such life. The living fraction of the soil is beneficial to making the soil a favorable place for plant roots to grow. These organisms live largely in the soil solution—the film of water around soil particles—and feed on dead organic matter, particularly the annual crop of dead grass roots. As a by-product of this decay accomplished by microbes, there are nutrients released for use by plant roots. Without the action of these millions of microscopic forms of life, soil would shortly become a poor place for roots to grow. The objective, therefore, is to promote the normal activity of these unseen microbes by proper turf management practices.

THE CYCLE OF SOIL NUTRIENTS

The microscopic forms of life in soils are responsible for what are termed the "cycles" of plant-food release. There is a cycle for each nutrient; the most important for grass is the nitrogen cycle. Nitrogen compounds are provided in the soil solution either by the decay of organic matter or through the application of fertilizers containing nitrogen. Nitrogen must be present either as nitrate or ammonia to be absorbed by plant roots. The plants convert this nitrogen into proteins, the complex part of the protoplasm in all cells that make up the living parts of the plant. After the death of a plant, or any portion (roots, stems, leaves) of a plant, this dead organic matter is decomposed by microbial action, and the nitrogen is released in soluble form for use by plants. If the soil becomes too waterlogged or too poorly aerated during the decay process, some nitrogen gas may be lost to the air. Also, the water-soluble compounds of nitrogen—principally the nitrates—are readily leached through soil into ground water by rainfall and irrigation. The nitrogen cycle is essentially a sequence of these events: (1) the absorption of soluble nitrogen compounds by growing plants, (2) the eventual death of plant parts, (3) the decay of dead tissues by microbes with release of soluble nitrogen compounds, and (4) the use again by plant roots. Since nitrogen is constantly being lost by water percolating through the soil or by nitrogen gas escaping at the soil surface, fertilizers containing nitrogen are added as needed to maintain a continually adequate supply for plant growth.

A similar cycle is going on with each of the other essential elements that plants absorb from the soil. Occasionally the microbes are releasing new supplies of these elements from their action on silt and clay particles, as well as by decay of organic matter. These elements, after being absorbed by plants, are restored to circulation upon the decay of dead parts by the soil microorganisms.

Even the humus in the soil is the product of the activity of soil microbes. The plant roots, stems, leaves, and other organic materials are not humus, nor can they produce the benefits associated with humus until they are broken down by microbial action. All organic materials must decompose before humus is produced. Were it not for the decay of the annual crops of grass roots, in a few years the soil would become so thoroughly filled with lifeless roots that healthy grass growth would be impossible. This condition does occur where roots have not decayed because of excessive soil acidity, inadequate nitrogen supply, or other causes. Correction of the soil acidity, or other causal factors that have prevented root decay by microbes, will release this organic matter so that it can enter the organic-matter cycle.

Obviously, it is highly desirable to maintain healthy conditions in the soil for microbial activity to ensure strong and durable turf. Experience shows that soil conditions of moisture, aeration, and nutrients that promote plant growth are the same conditions that soil microorganisms prefer for their growth. Consequently, one may generally take for granted that microbial life in the soil will be satisfactory if favorable conditions have been provided for grass roots. In other words, nature will take care of the biological or living parts of the soil processes if man provides the physical and chemical conditions in soil required for plant growth.

In conclusion, it is well to remember that at least half, and often more than half, of the grass plant is below the surface of the soil. Unless conditions are satisfactory for grass roots, it is impossible to have healthy, satisfactory turf. Appropriate attention to the underground part of the grass will greatly simplify the task of adequate turf maintenance.

EXPLANATION OF TECHNICAL TERMS

- **Aeration** is the movement of air into the soil mass through openings between soil particles. Some movement of air occurs because of differences in temperature between soil and atmosphere. Water movements into and out of soil also induce aeration. Any form of tillage or mechanical disturbance of the soil improves the aeration by enlarging the porosity of the soil. Compaction caused by tramping or traffic on soggy soils greatly reduces aeration. Water logged soil excludes air, and roots are thus deprived of the oxygen needed for their growth.

- **Colloids** in soils are mostly composed of clay particles or well-decomposed organic matter. The colloid particles are so small that when dispersed in water they remain suspended for long periods. In soils, the colloids usually are clustered around silt and sand particles. The colloids are responsible for a large part of the water-holding capacity of the soil and for the supply of nutrient elements taken up by roots.

- **Nutrients** are the substances taken up from soil that are required for normal plant growth. Strictly speaking, oxygen and water are nutrients, but generally the term is applied to soluble forms of nitrogen, phosphorus and potassium. However, calcium and magnesium oxides and sulfate compounds are also nutrients. The trace elements needed in very small amounts by plants—iron, manganese, zinc, copper, boron and molybdenum—are also nutrients.

- **Parent material** is the earthy material lying below the true soil produced by long weathering. In undisturbed soil there is a true topsoil at the surface and below this the partially weathered subsoil, both overlying the parent earthy material. Where there has been extensive movement of soil during grading and construction, the parent material may be left at the surface or mingled with the topsoil and subsoil. Parent materials contain no soil humus and are generally light-colored.

- **Soil texture** refers to the proportions of sand, silt, and clay present in the soil. A soil with limited amounts of silt and clay is termed sandy loam. As the amounts of silt and clay increase, the soils are termed loam, silt loam, clay loam or clay soil.

- **Soil structure** refers to the degree of porosity or tilth that a soil possesses. The soil particles—sand, silt, and clay—are usually intermingled and form granules or aggregates. A soil in good tilth has granules separated by pore spaces that are occupied by air and water. Heavy-textured soils are more likely to become compacted and have poor structure, thus limiting aeration, water-holding capacity, and ability of the soil to supply nutrients to plant roots.

- **Subsoil** is the layer of earth lying below the true topsoil in which weathering and root penetrations have occurred to some extent. However, subsoil is generally much lighter in color and less fertile than topsoil.

- **Topsoil** is the layer of soil at the surface in which there is the greatest accumulation of humus and the greatest degree of weathering. Topsoil is considerably darker in color than subsoil. It is potentially more fertile, but may require fertilizer, lime, and other amendments to meet the needs of turf plants. In arid regions, topsoil is often light colored and has about the same value for plant growth as the underlying subsoil. In river bottoms and other alluvial deposits, there may be little or no difference between topsoil and subsoil.

Chapter 6

SOIL ACIDITY AND LIMING

OCCURRENCE OF SOIL ACIDITY

Soil acidity is similar in all regions that have abundant rainfall (see Figure 1-1). These include the *cool humid region*, the *warm humid region*, and the *North Pacific Coastal region*. Most of these soils are too acidic to grow good turf unless their acidity is corrected by liming. Though some grasses are more tolerant of soil acidity than others, the adverse effects of soil acidity on the soil itself are universal. Correction of soil acidity is simple and safe.

SOIL ACIDITY AND IMPERMEABILITY

One important effect of soil acidity is its strong tendency to make the soil impermeable to moisture. Acid soils are more likely to become dry in periods of drought since rainfall, particularly in thunderstorms, will run off rather than penetrate the soil.

SOIL ACIDITY AND ROOT BOUND TURF

A second adverse effect of soil acidity is an accumulation of dead but undecomposed grass roots, which produce a root bound condition. Strong soil acidity interferes with normal root decay. In some carefully conducted experiments at the New Jersey Agricultural Experiment Station, it was found that strongly acid soils accumulated 10 times more roots in the upper foot of soil when compared to adjoining soil areas where acidity had been corrected by liming. This accumulation of roots in root bound sod can retard the penetration of water from rain into the soil.

SOIL ACIDITY AND TOXIC MINERAL COMPOUNDS

Acid soils have a high content of soluble forms of aluminum, manganese and iron compounds that are toxic to turfgrasses. These elements rapidly react with the *phosphates* applied to turf and make the phosphate insoluble and unavailable to grass roots. Thus, plants may starve for phosphates in spite of continued feeding.

SOIL ACIDITY AND FERTILIZER NITROGEN

Turfgrasses have difficulty absorbing nitrogen in the form of ammonia where soils are strongly acidic. Most commercial fertilizers contain nitrogen in ammonia form as ammonium sulfate or as urea. On acid soils, the ammonia accumulates in the soil and the portion that does enter the roots

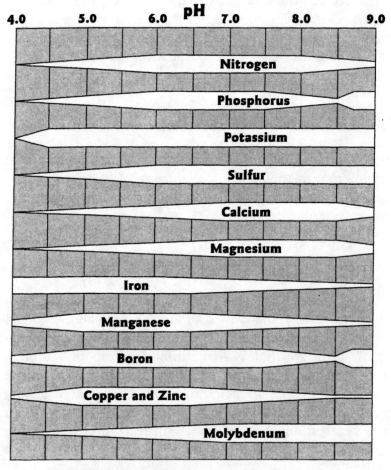

Figure 6-1. Nutrient availability in relation to soil pH. The width of the bar shows the relative availability of each element with a change in soil reaction (pH).

is quite toxic. Plants that have too much unassimilated ammonia in their tissues become dark bluish green in color, and growth practically ceases. In advanced stages of injury, leaves become brown at the tips.

SOIL REACTION AND THE AVAILABILITY OF PLANT NUTRIENTS

Figure 6-1 illustrates the effect of soil reaction (degree of acidity or alkalinity) on the availability of essential nutrients in the soil. The width of the bar for each nutrient shows the relative availability of each element at different soil reactions. Six elements are required by plants in large amounts—nitrogen, phosphorus, potassium, sulfur, calcium, and magnesium. These nutrients are most availability in the range from slightly acid to slightly alkaline.

The trace elements (iron, manganese, boron, copper, and zinc) are needed in very small amounts and can become excessively soluble in strongly acid soils and quite toxic to plant roots. Correction of soil acidity is necessary to avoid such toxicity.

REASONS FOR SOIL ACIDITY

Why do soils become acid? Knowing the answer helps in planning regular turf care. One major cause is rainfall and irrigation that gradually leach out the calcium and magnesium found in the soil materials. Leaching leaves behind the acidic portions of these soil materials. These losses occur at a higher rate in warm periods than in cool periods, and thus they are greater in warmer climates.

Calcium and magnesium are the basic materials in limestone; therefore, if the original rocks that formed the soils were limestone, the dangers of acidity are lessened. Soils derived from granite, shale, or other non-lime-bearing materials are usually not acidic. Sandy and other coarse-textured soils are not acidic.

Use of Acid-forming Fertilizers

Another reason for the creation of soil acidity is the use of fertilizers that have an acid reaction. All fertilizers that provide nitrogen in the form of ammonia or that are converted to ammonia in the soil will leave an acid residue in the soil. In the case of sulfate of ammonia, the ammonia

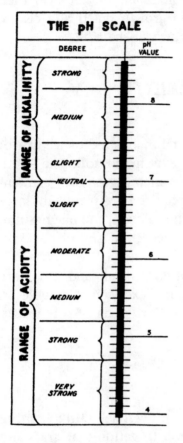

Figure 6-2. The pH scale showing the ranges of soil acidity and alkalinity at which plants grow. (Courtesy, National Lime Association)

is absorbed more rapidly than the sulfate, and the acid-forming sulfate accumulates in the soil.

MEASURING SOIL ACIDITY

Acidity or alkalinity is measured on a pH scale of 1-14. Soil pH is actually a measurement of the concentration of hydrogen ions (H+) in the soil solution. This is analogous to a ruler used to measure length, as illustrated in Figure 6-2.

CORRECTING SOIL ACIDITY

Correcting acidity is simple. Outside the humid regions, liming is not needed since the soils are not acid but are alkaline. In humid regions where lime has been added in abundance, the soils may be alkaline. Turfgrasses grow best at pH values of 6.0 to 8.0. pH values below 5.5 have adverse effects on both soils and plants, and values below 5.0 suggest real trouble.

Most soil-testing kits will measure soil pH quickly. They are not expensive and are reasonably accurate if instructions are followed carefully. An alternative is to take a representative sample to a reliable soil testing laboratory for analysis. The results may be expressed as pH values and in terms of lime requirements to correct acidity.

Finely Ground Limestone

The material for correction of soil acidity is finely ground limestone. Since it is used in agriculture, it is often termed "agricultural limestone." Limestone should be very finely ground to be fully satisfactory; if coarsely ground, the reaction rate is very slow. It may vary widely in color from nearly white to dark gray without affecting its value as a neutralizing material. It is safe for both humans and animals and quite easy to use. Finely ground limestone does not cake together when applied to turf but sifts through grass when applied as topdressing. Finely ground limestone moves downward into soil under the influence of rain or irrigation water, but not laterally in the soil.

One important point is that considerable time is required for limestone to correct soil acidity. Even in warm, moist soils, months are required for enough of the lime to dissolve to accomplish neutralization of the soil acidity. Thus, liming should be done ahead of actual need. This slowness of action has some good features. It means that a single application, if made in sufficient amounts, will prevent excessive soil acidity for as much as two years.

Lime for New Seedings

In preparing a seedbed for new planting, lime should be thoroughly mixed throughout the soil layers in which grass roots are expected to develop. It is true that the influence of lime applied to the surface will gradually move downward with time, but prompt correction of acidity to a depth of 6 to 12 inches requires mixing of limestone to those depths. Rapid development of new seedling roots requires correction of excessive acidity throughout the soil mass. The need for deep liming depends on the initial acidity of the soil being used. Limestone does not move laterally; therefore, every square inch of soil surface should be limed to produce uniform results.

Figure 6-3. A small spreader that will handle all types of dry materials.
(Courtesy, Danville Area Community College)

Time of Application

Ground limestone may be applied at any convenient time, during any season of the year. It is best to apply it when grass leaves are dry so the material will sift down to the soil. Watering immediately after spreading not only washes the dust off the leaves, but also carries material into the moist soil where action can begin. In cooler regions, liming is done in fall, winter, or spring. Successive freezing and thawing of the soil will speed the penetration of the lime.

The action of limestone is always slow, and the full benefits of liming will not become evident until months after application. Thus, fall liming is important if corrective effects are needed for the following growing season. Watering or rainfall will aid in carrying limestone into the soil and speed up the correction of soil acidity. Once limestone has been applied to the soil the gradual release of calcium and magnesium to correct acidity will continue for two to three years.

Amounts of Limestone to Use

Two kinds of information are needed to apply limestone effectively: (1) the area of the grounds or turf to be treated and (2) the degree of soil acidity. The area should be measured in feet, and expressed in terms of thousands of square feet. A lawn area 40 feet long by 50 feet wide will contain two thousand square feet of turf (40 × 50 feet = 2,000 square feet). To measure odd-shaped areas, divide them into geometric blocks, figure out each area separately, and add the results. Since the size of the turf area will be needed to determine amounts of fertilizer, seed, and pesticide, make a record of the size of each turf area for future reference.

The degree of soil acidity is found by an actual soil test. If different portions of the lawn have different kinds of soil or have had a history of different treatments, it is well to test each turf area separately. Remember that no test is any more accurate than the sample tested. Taking a representative sample is simple. Use a clean pail to receive soil, and with a clean trowel or sharp spade take a small slice of soil to a depth of at least four inches. Do not include trash or organic matter at the surface. A dozen or more slices will be needed for each area. Mix the samples together to provide a composite sample. Not more than a cupful is needed to make the soil test.

More lime is required to correct acidity on loams and clay loams than on sandy soils since the heavier textures have greater amounts of acidity. This has advantages, since heavier soils once limed will become acidic more slowly than sandy soils. In other words, light-textured soils change in reaction to limestone more rapidly, but they also lose their lime more rapidly.

Table 6-1 gives a convenient guide to the amounts of limestone to use in correcting soil acidity. When topdressing established lawns, heavy applications should not be made at one time to correct all of the acidity. For established turf 50 to 75 pounds of limestone per 1,000 square feet should be used for the first application, and repeated every six months until the total amount needed has been applied. Very heavy topdressing of lawns on strongly acid soils sometimes interferes with plant nutrition and causes the grass to lose greenness. This may persist for some weeks before recovery occurs because lime moves downward but not laterally. Lime spread evenly over the soil surface will produce uniform results. Mixing with soil wherever possible hastens the effects.

Liming Extensive Areas

Some turf areas are extensive enough to be measured in acres. An acre contains 43,560 square feet. To approximate the total lime requirement on an acre basis, multiply the amounts shown in Table 6-1 by 43.5 to get the

Table 6-1
Pounds of Finely Ground Limestone Required to Correct Soil Acidity

Soil Reaction		Pounds of Limestone per 1,000 Square Feet of Lawn Area			
pH	Condition	Light Sandy Soils	Medium Sandy Loams	Loams and Silt Loams	Clay Loams and Clay Soils
4.0	Excessively acid	90	120	165	200
4.5	Very strongly acid	80	105	150	180
5.0	Strongly acid	70	90	120	150
5.5	Moderately acid	45	60	90	120
6.0	Slightly acid	25	30	45	60
6.5	Slightly acid	none	none	none	none
7.0	Neutral	none	none	none	none
7.5	Mildly alkaline	none	none	none	none
8.0	Moderately alkaline	none	none	none	none

pounds needed per acre. Thus, a medium loam with a pH of 5.5 will require 60 pounds × 43.5 (2,610 pounds) of lime per acre. When large areas are treated, it is customary to express limestone requirements in tons per acre. For this example apply 1.25 tons of limestone per acre to achieve the desired state of soil reaction.

Soil acidity is continually developing in all humid regions. To avoid trouble, soil tests should be made annually to determine lime needs. There are several important fringe benefits that accompany the proper use of limestone. Not only does it increase the vigor of the turfgrasses, but it also reduces weed problems and makes the turf more resistant to diseases and insect pests.

ERRONEOUS CLAIMS ABOUT SOIL ACIDITY

Beware of the erroneous claims that turfgrasses are not sensitive to soil acidity and that soil acidity helps in weed control. Scientific evidence does not support these claims; nor does it support the assertions that fertilizers replace proper liming. It is true that some grasses are more tolerant of soil acidity than others, but all turfgrasses will be sturdier on soils that are not strongly acidic. As to weed control, some of the most

Figure 6-4. When liming extensive areas, it may be necessary to handle materials in bulk. (Courtesy, South Side Country Club)

serious weeds (such as crabgrass, chickweed, and nutgrass) are more tolerant of soil acidity than turfgrasses. Where soil acidity goes uncorrected, such weeds spread at the expense of the grass. For example, crabgrass thrives on acid soils wherever there is sufficient moisture.

Making soil conditions favorable for the desired turfgrass is an important step in a weed control program. With liming, proper fertilizing, correct watering, and good mowing practices, weeds don't have to be a problem. When given an opportunity for vigorous growth, adapted turfgrasses offer very severe competition to weeds for space, moisture, and nutrients. Further information on these conditions will be found in subsequent chapters of this book.

Remember: Limestone is inexpensive, safe to use, and may be applied in almost any season. Skimping on liming is poor economy.

EXPLANATION OF TECHNICAL TERMS

- **Soil acidity** refers to the amount of acid substance in the thin film of water surrounding soil particles. The acid is actually created by hydrogen ions, which are not immediately neutralized by calcium or magnesium ions.

- **Soil alkalinity** refers to the amount of alkaline (the opposite of acid) substances in the films of soil water. The alkaline ions (OH) are responsible for alkaline conditions.

- **Soil reaction** is the general term that refers to the entire range of conditions from acid to alkaline. The soil reaction is measured in pH units. Neutral pH is 7.0. Values below 7.0 are increasingly acid, and values above 7.0 are increasingly alkaline.

- **Soil pH** refers to the concentration of hydrogen ions in the soil solution. At pH 7.0, the amounts of hydrogen ions (H+) are balanced by the hydroxyl ions, (OH–) and the reaction is neutral. The degree of acidity and of alkalinity is usually expressed in pH units by soil testing laboratories.

Chapter 7

PRACTICAL USE OF FERTILIZERS ON TURF

FEEDING TURFGRASSES

Turfgrasses used for home lawns, golf courses, and playing fields must have a liberal supply of the essential nutrients in a balanced ratio if they are to be vigorous and capable of withstanding turf use. These essential elements should be in adequate supply throughout the full growing season. Since these elements are essential for growth, a deficiency in any one of them determines total growth. Fortunately, the soil and its humus content serve as a reservoir for nutrients that are tapped by the grass's root system. Fertilization practices should replenish this reservoir as needed. Such re-

Figure 7-1.   Rotary spreader for rapid coverage of small- to medium-size areas applying a wide range of dry materials.

plenishment should recognize the current reserves in the soil and also the anticipated needs of the grass in the months ahead.

ESSENTIAL NUTRIENT ELEMENTS

The essential nutrient elements that must be available to grass roots are *nitrogen, phosphorus, potassium, calcium, magnesium,* and *sulfur. Iron* is also needed but in such small amounts that soils generally provide an adequate supply without any additions. *Calcium* and *magnesium* are best provided by liming when soils are acid. If soils are not acid, the supplies of calcium and magnesium inherently present in the soil are almost invariably adequate. *Sulfur* is usually supplied in fertilizers as an incidental component of phosphate fertilizers. However, with the growing use of concentrated and purified phosphates it is becoming more common for the sulfur supply to be inadequate, particularly when turf is established and maintained on raw soil materials low in humus supply.

THE NUTRIENT CYCLE

The soil is not an inert substance into which fertilizers, organic materials, and soil amendments are placed for plant use. It is a constantly changing and complex body with materials slowly dissolving from the clay and silt particles into the film of water around every particle. Fertilizers and other soluble amendments added to the soil may remain in solution in the films of soil water or they may react with the solid clay and silt and produce insoluble materials that become part of the framework of the soil. Within the films of soil water live large numbers of bacteria, molds, and protozoa. This living fraction of the soil is constantly decomposing the dead roots, stems, and leaves and also lifeless insects, worms, protozoa, and other microbes. The decay of these organic materials releases the component substances in simple forms. Decay is particularly important in replenishing the supply of nutrients that were tied up in the organic substances. Living soil microbes also dissolves small amounts of essential plant nutrients out of the clay and silt particles.

MICROBIAL ACTIVITY IN SOILS

Fertile soils have active populations of microbes and other soil-inhabiting life (worms, larvae, etc.). These supplies of organic substances serve as the source of energy for the soil populations. Since grass produce an annual crop of roots, their decay under proper soil conditions is a constant source of nutrients. This process completes a cycle in the circulation of nutrients: (1) uptake from soil water of the nutrients from fertilizers or decaying organic matter; (2) growth of grass; (3) death of plant parts; and (4) decay and return of nutrients to the soil solution.

Decay of organic materials is slow, but as temperatures increase so does the decomposition rate. When the soil temperature drops below 45°F this decomposition practically ceases. Part of the organic matter is more resistant and accumulates in a transitory material such as *soil humus*. Humus itself decomposes slowly during warm weather under conditions of adequate aeration, moisture, and freedom from excessive acidity. Thus, soils rich in humus have an increased nutrient-supplying power for grass growth over those deficient in humus.

Soils will differ in their ability to supply nutrients to plants. Soils with high humus content will supply more of the necessary nutrients for turf growth. For soils without such an ideal make up, good management practices can compensate for inherent weaknesses. Lawns, parks, and playing fields that are planted on subsoils will require liberal fertilization for healthy growth of turfgrasses.

KINDS OF FERTILIZERS

The big three elements necessary for good turfgrass growth are nitrogen, phosphorus, and potassium. The elements are supplied as chemical compounds of the essential element. Nitrogen is called *organic nitrogen, nitrates,* or *ammonia*. Phosphorus is termed *phosphates*. Potassium is known as *potash*.

Organic Fertilizers

It is a well-recognized principle that plants can absorb only nutrients that are dissolved in water. The value of organic materials depends on their decomposition and the amounts of nutrients present in the materials. Nitrogen is the primary nutrient in organic materials. Organic materials used for fertilizers fall into two groups—natural substances and those produced synthetically. The natural substances are usually animal manures, sewage sludge, and seed meals. The actual fertilizer value of such materials is determined by the percentage of total nitrogen. This is required by law to be expressed in percentage of *nitrogen* in actual dry matter. Processed sewage sludge is widely used and marketed under various trade names.

Since the decay of natural organic materials occurs primarily in periods of warm weather, this class of fertilizers has definite limitations as the sole source of nutrients for feeding grass. The nutrients in organic fertilizers are gradually released during the growing season rather than being available all at once as with completely soluble fertilizers. Moreover, the nutrients (particularly phosphates) released by the decay of organic fertilizers do not react quickly with soil to become unavailable.

Synthetic Organic Fertilizers

Since 1960, several slow release nitrogen sources have been developed. These fertilizers give the turf manager the opportunity to apply nitrogen less often than in the past but without the worry of burning the turf. New nitrogen sources are synthetic (man-made). Ureaformaldehyde (UF), methylene urea, sulfur-coated urea (SCU), and isobutylidene diurea (IBDU) are examples of slowly-available nitrogen carriers.

Ureaformaldehyde is manufactured by treating urea (45 percent nitrogen) with different amounts of formaldehyde (formalin). Untreated urea is completely water soluble and promptly breaks down in the soil to form *ammonia*, which may either be absorbed by plant roots or converted by microbes to *nitrate*, which also is soluble and absorbed readily by roots.

Figure 7-2. A PTO operated rotary spreader for rapid coverage of extensive areas. (Courtesy, J. Michael Hart)

When small amounts of formaldehyde are added to urea solutions, new compounds are formed that are termed *ureaform*.

Actually, there is a whole family of ureaform compounds that may be produced, depending on the proportion of formaldehyde reacted with the urea. As the proportion of formaldehyde in the ureaform fertilizer increases the solubility of the ureaform decreases. As the proportion of formaldehyde increases the resulting compound is less soluble.

Other Nitrogen Fertilizers

Other sources of nitrogen for the turf manager are *sulfate of ammonia* (21 percent nitrogen), *ammonium nitrate* (33 percent nitrogen), and *urea* (42 to 46 percent nitrogen). These are water soluble and readily taken up by plant roots. However, their individual usefulness is not always the same. Sulfate of ammonia has a strong tendency to make soils acidic and should be used on soils that are not acidic. Ammonium nitrate and urea are mildly acid-forming and are more effective than sulfate of ammonia for general turf use. Because these nitrogen sources are water soluble, they release nitrogen almost as soon as they are applied. This quick release can cause very quick, lush grass growth that may not be wanted. Soluble nitrogen fertilizers also have a greater potential for burning the turf leaf after application. Use lower rates of application and water the turf after applying any of these nitrogen carriers. Another precaution to remember when applying these soluble nitrogen carrier fertilizers is to apply to dry grass leaves.

Since the value of a nitrogen fertilizer is dependent on the amount of actual nitrogen supplied, it is important to note the percentage of nitrogen contained. By law, this percentage must be plainly shown on all packages of nitrogen fertilizer. One pound of urea (45 percent nitrogen) carries as much nitrogen as two pounds of sulfate of ammonia (21 percent nitrogen). Fertilizers must enter the soil and remain in the root feeding zone to help plants grow.

Materials added to the soil tend to move straight downward and do not spread out laterally. Thus, fertilizers should be spread as uniformly as possible over the ground surface. Spots or strips that receive no fertilizer will derive no benefit from adjoining treated areas. Grass on the missed spots and strips will be lighter in color.

Soluble nitrogen fertilizers of these types have the disadvantage of moving all the way through the soil profile with the passage of water, below the root feeding zone. Obviously, these losses of nitrogen are most likely to be serious under conditions of continued heavy watering or rainfall and are most acute on sandy or open-textured soils. To maintain a continuing supply of available nitrogen in the root zones apply soluble nitrogen fertilizers periodically in smaller amounts. This characteristic of soluble fertilizer can sometimes be an asset, as with inadvertent over fertilization. Heavy watering to wash the excess of soluble salts through the soil profile is one way to deal with such accidents as spillage on small area.

Commercially Mixed Fertilizers

Mixed fertilizers must show the guaranteed percentage of each nutrient in the bag. These constituents are reported by long-established practice in terms of percentage by weight of *nitrogen* (N), *phosphate* (P_2O_5 equivalent), and *potash* (K_2O equivalent). Chemists have long complained that this method of expressing plant food content is neither accurate nor logical since the elements are not present in these forms. It is also true that all three substances are nearly always necessary for stimulating vigorous growth, and the needs of a plant are easily met by varying the ratios of these elements in the kind of fertilizers applied.

Nitrogen. Nitrogen is needed in the greatest amounts by all plants except legumes. Legumes, such as clover, can transform inert nitrogen from soil air into usable compounds. Nitrogen occurs as a vital part of the protoplasm

Figure 7-3. Inside storage of fertilizer may be required when purchasing on a periodic basis. (Courtesy, South Side Country Club)

of every living cell; without it, new growth is impossible. When nitrogen supply is deficient, the leaves turn light green or greenish-yellow from lack of chlorophyll production. An excess of nitrogen produces a tender succulent growth that is susceptible to disease damage.

Phosphates. Phosphates are also present in the nucleus of every living cell although in smaller amounts than nitrogen. An inadequate supply can retard or may halt growth, particularly of roots. Unlike nitrogen deficiency, there are no clear-cut visible symptoms of phosphate deficiency. A reduction in root growth is typical of phosphate deficiency but other conditions may produce the same effect. Phosphates are very important for the development of roots on newly seeded turf areas. Good starter fertilizers have a higher percentage of phosphate than maintenance fertilizers. Phosphates move slowly in the soil and fertilizer phosphates may be converted to an unavailable form by chemical reaction with clay and silt.

Potash. Potash (potassium) is also important for healthy plants as well as for vigorous growth. Potassium occurs principally in leaves, where it is an important factor in the manufacture of sugars, starches, and proteins. It is essential for the movement of foods between tissues and organs. Potassium is rarely present in soils in amounts sufficient to meet plant needs. Potash may be stored in the soil in available form. A soil test is the best guide to find the current level of potash in the soil. The soil test can also suggest the need for a potash application. The symptoms of potash deficiency are browning of leaf margins and tips. These symptoms are difficult to see on regularly cut turf. Without a soil test, a serious potash deficiency may go unnoticed.

HOW TO EVALUATE A FERTILIZER

For more than a half century, the law has required that the actual percentage of nutrient elements be clearly shown on fertilizer bags. There are no *miracle substances* in the fertilizer package, though the advertising claims might lead the buyer to think so. The actual value of any fertilizers is determined by the percentage composition of available *nitrogen, phosphate,* and *potash.*

Law requires the nutrient content to be expressed as percentage by weight of nitrogen (N), phosphate (P_2O_5), and potash (K_2O). The label reading 25-5-10 means that it contains 25 pounds of nitrogen, 5 pounds of phosphate, and 10 pounds of potash per 100 pounds of total weight.

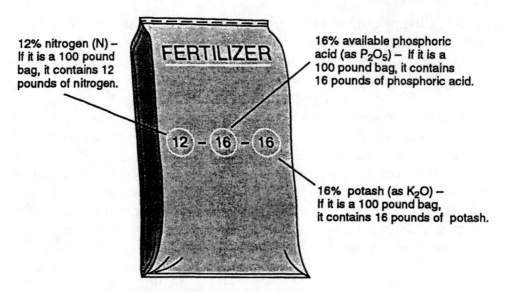

12% nitrogen (N) –
If it is a 100 pound
bag, it contains 12
pounds of nitrogen.

16% available phosphoric
acid (as P_2O_5) – If it is a
100 pound bag, it contains
16 pounds of phosphoric acid.

16% potash (as K_2O) –
If it is a 100 pound bag,
it contains 16 pounds of potash.

Figure 7-4. When evaluating fertilizer, look for the numerals on the bag.

The relationship of nitrogen, phosphorus, and potassium in the bag is often called the nutrient ratio. Turfgrass needs five times more nitrogen than phosphorus and twice as much potassium as phosphorus. The nutrient ratio of 5 to 1 to 2 is considered best. The relative quantity of each of these three nutrients is much more important than the total nitrogen, phosphorus, or potassium in the bag. Good turf maintenance fertilizers should have a ratio of 5-1-2 to 8-1-2. To find the nutrient ratio in a bag of fertilizer, divide the phosphorus percentage into the nitrogen percentage and divide the phosphorus percentage into the potassium percentage. For example, a bag of fertilizer has an analysis of 24-4-8: divide 24 by 4 (6); divide 4 by 4 (1); and divide 8 by 4 (2); thus the ratio is 6-1-2.

To evaluate the fertilizer, look for the guaranteed analysis that must be shown in numerals on the bag. If the buyer knows what kind of fertilizer is needed for his grass, he need not try to evaluate the advertising claims made on the package nor its eye appeal. The guaranteed analysis is provided for the protection and guidance of the buyer.

FERTILIZER FOR NEW PLANTINGS

Soil samples of each area to be planted should be taken and tested to determine the needs for lime, phosphate, and potash. The fertilizer needs will be influenced by soil acidity. If the soil acidity is about pH 5.5 the addition of lime, as shown by a soil test, is an important companion treatment. Unless the root zone is made favorable for root growth, the turfgrasses may be weakened by inability to occupy more than the surface inch or two. As a general guideline, apply 8 to 10 pounds of a 12-25-13 starter fertilizer to each 1,000 square feet of turf area. Three-fourths of the total amount should be mixed through the soil, and the remaining one-fourth should be spread and worked into the upper inch of soil. A slowly available form of nitrogen should be used. The use of phosphate, potash and lime should not be skimped at this stage since this is by far the best time to improve the soil of the future root zone.

FERTILIZING ESTABLISHED TURF

Cool-Season Grasses

Healthy grass generally requires a yearly fertilization regime to insure a continuous supply of nitrogen, phosphate, and potash throughout the growing season. For all cool-season grasses (bluegrass, fescue, bentgrass, ryegrass), an early fall application is important. This permits the grasses to continue growth much later into the cool season (when warm-season weeds such as crabgrass are not competitive). During this season food reserves are stored in the crowns, and next year's new shoots develop. A

Figure 7-5. Spreading fertilizer on rough-graded soil in preparation for a new planting. (Courtesy, Danville Area Community College)

similar fertilizer application in very early spring will give the cool-season grasses a head start in growth at the time when the weather is most favorable. A late fall fertilization, called a dormant fertilization, is now recommended by many turf specialists. Even after the top growth has stopped for the season the turfgrass roots continue to grow until the ground freezes. This increase in root growth without increasing the top growth will provide the turf plant with a root system that will better withstand adverse environmental conditions in the coming year. Two applications of fertilizer in the spring are recommended for most home lawns. An early application made in March will start the turfgrass spring growth. A second application made around Memorial Day will provide the lawn with the nutrients to continue growth through the summer.

Warm-Season Grasses

For warm-season grasses (bermudagrass, carpetgrass, centipedegrass, St. Augustinegrass), the kinds of fertilizer may be the same as for cool-season grasses, but the season of application should be adjusted to the growing season of the grasses. Early spring and midsummer are preferred times of application to maintain a continuous supply of nutrients for these species. It is perhaps even more important to supply one-half or more of the nitrogen in a slowly available form in warmer climates. Nitrogen is lost or exhausted more rapidly at higher temperatures, particularly under abundant watering and rainfall. Sandy and open-textured soils lose nitrogen quite rapidly when it is supplied in water-soluble form.

EXPLANATION OF TECHNICAL TERMS

- **Nutrient cycle** refers to the sequence of events that normally occurs in the growth of plants. Their ultimate death, followed by decay, releases the nutrients for absorption by plants. The details of the nitrogen cycle are different from the phosphorus cycle and the potassium cycle because of the differing properties of each element and its compounds. However, the general sequence is much the same for all nutrient elements. The addition of fertilizers generally increases the supply of nutrients that are involved in the cycle. Removal of tops reduces the amount of nutrients in the cycle.

- **Commercial fertilizers** were originally given this name to distinguish them from animal manures and other natural substances such as guano, seed meals, and slaughterhouse wastes. They are composed of inorganic chemical substances or mixtures carrying nitrogen, phosphorus, and potassium. However, urea and ureaform compounds are organic in nature. These materials now make up a major part of most commercial fertilizers.

- **Mineral fertilizers** are the chemical compounds that carry essential plant nutrients. For *nitrogen*, these are principally nitrate or ammonium compounds or urea that rapidly breaks down into ammonia. For *phosphorus*, the usual material is some form of phosphate produced by treating natural rock phosphate with acid. For *potassium*, the chemical is mostly potassium chloride or potassium sulfate. These materials are mixed in different proportions to produce the type of fertilizer needed.

- **Organic fertilizers** are of plant or animal origin such as seed meals, tankage, sewage sludge, guano, and manure. As noted under "commercial fertilizers," urea and ureaform compounds are technically organic in nature. Natural organic fertilizers release the nutrients contained only upon decomposition. Therefore, the release is extended over a long period. By contrast, the mineral fertilizers are mostly soluble and the nutrients are immediately available. Ureaform compounds may be formulated to release part of the nitrogen at once and the remainder over an extended period.

- **Microbe** is a general term used to include all small organisms that can only be seen with a microscope. These forms include bacteria, viruses, actinomyces, fungi, and protozoa. Soil microbes live in the thin film of water surrounding soil particles and granules and are active in decomposing all kinds of organic substances.

- **Soil humus** is the name given to partially decomposed plant and animal remains in the soil. This resistant fraction of organic substances becomes redistributed through the soil mass around soil particles and granules. The humus layers are quite thin but very important in acting as a weak "cement, or bonding agent. Humus is responsible for the dark coloration of topsoil. Soil humus is subject to further slow decay when the temperature and the amount of moisture are favorable.

Chapter 8

PLANTING NEW TURF

METHODS OF ESTABLISHING TURFGRASSES

There are four commonly used methods of establishing turfgrasses: (1) seeding, (2) plugging, (3) sodding, and (4) sprigging. Establishment by seeding is the most commonly used, and it is usually the least expensive of the four methods. Sprigging is a way of establishing certain warm season species and strains that do not produce viable seeds. These warm region grasses include improved strains of turf types of bermudagrass, zoysia grass, St. Augustinegrass, and centipedegrass.

Seasons For Planting New Turf Propagation By Seed

In establishing turf from seed, four factors are necessary for seed germination: (1) live seed, (2) adequate moisture, (3) sufficient soil warmth, and (4) adequate aeration. If one or more of these factors are not present the seed will not germinate or the plant will be too weak to survive.

Early Stages of Germination

Viable seeds are capable of germination. This is determined by actual germination testing in a laboratory. Since live and dead seeds look alike, state and federal laws require that all seed labels show the percentage germination of the species in the package and the date when tested. During storage, grass seed may rapidly lose viability. Only purchase seed tested within the current year.

SEEDING NEW TURF

The success of any new planting depends largely on the preparations that are made before planting.

81

Figure 8-1. A grass breeding nursery. The white bags prevent cross-pollination. The progeny from these grass heads will be planted in solid plots to determine their usefulness for turf. (Courtesy, The Pennsylvania State University)

- **Choosing grasses**—The grasses should be suited to the climatic zone and soil conditions. If the areas to be seeded are partially shaded, the selected grasses must be shade tolerant. The grasses should be capable of thriving under the management practices that are intended, such as height and frequency of cutting, fertilization, and watering.

- **Soil preparation**—The soil should be prepared for planting by correcting drainage problems, adjusting the soil acidity, incorporating fertilizer, adding organic matter, and final smoothing of the surface.

The selection of grasses may suggest species that are propagated vegetatively by sprigging, plugging, or sodding. However, the soil preparation steps will be the same for the establishment of a new lawn either by seed or vegetative means. The unique features of vegetative plantings will be discussed later in this chapter under the heading "Vegetative Planting of New Turf."

In the cooler regions there are two preferred seasons—early fall and early spring. Spring seeding should be done as early as possible to allow the seedlings to become well established before hot weather occurs and to minimize the invasion by summer weeds. Very often a better time for new seedlings is in late summer or early fall. The summer weeds are not a serious problem in such plantings because temperatures and rainfall are more often favorable for the grass. Cool-season grasses will survive winter temperatures if they become well established before freezing occurs. However, in new construction, the turf manager may find it necessary to plant whenever the area becomes available, irrespective of preferred planting dates. In such situations, special efforts are needed to minimize the hazards due to off-season planting. Light surface mulching with straw and careful watering will help protect new seedlings from heat and surface drying if planting occurs in late spring and early summer. Permanent plantings usually are not successful in midsummer, and good judgment may dictate postponement until late August. When a temporary, green cover is imperative, a seeding of ryegrass will give temporary occupancy until the season for permanent plantings arrives.

In the warmer regions, the preferred season is in the spring when temperatures are warm enough to allow established turf to turn green. Such early planting permits a full season of growth before cool-weather dormancy occurs. The turf manager in the warmer regions has a wide choice of planting periods.

Seed Mixtures and Blends for Cool Regions

A seed blend is made by combining two or more cultivars of a single grass species. Baron and Adelphi, which are both cultivars of Kentucky bluegrass (*Poa pratensis*), can be combined to make a Kentucky bluegrass blend. Seed mixtures, however, are a combination of two or more different species of turfgrass. A mixture containing perennial ryegrass and Kentucky bluegrass seed is a very popular mix where a mixture of different grass species is more likely to give satisfactory results than a single species. (Such mixtures are rarely used in the warmer regions since most of the better turfgrasses are planted by vegetative techniques rather than by seed.) For cooler regions, mixtures of adapted grasses have several advantages. Each of the component grasses differs in their seasons of most active growth, therefore, a mixture provides more uniform growth from early spring to late fall. Mixtures also provide some insurance against diseases, since disorders that attack one grass usually do not thrive on another species. Mixtures thus prevent the rapid spread of diseases and reduce total damage.

Today most seed mixture for cooler regions will contain a blend of two or three improved Kentucky bluegrass cultivars and a blend of two or three improved perennial ryegrass cultivars in about equal proportion by weight. For partially shaded turf, add 25 percent by weight of an improved cultivar of red fescue may be added to the grass seed mix with a reduction of the percentage of Kentucky bluegrass seed.

Figure 8-2.   A turf test plot with various grass seed types. (Courtesy, Terra
International, Inc., Professional Products)

Seed Quality

The turf manager has two choices as to grass-seed mixtures; purchase
the individual grasses and make up a mixture to meet the specific needs
of the site to be planted or seek commercial mixtures that will approximate
the estimated needs. However, today most turf managers purchase a seed
mixture from a seed supply company. The seed label must show each
species, *percent germination, percent purity*, and *date of testing* for each grass
present in the bag. The percentages of weed seed and of inert matter (trash
and dirt) in the mixture must also be shown on the seed package or label.

Besides total percentage of pure grass seed, the amount of weed seeds
present may be important, particularly if these weeds are serious pests.
Although grass seeds are all small, they vary greatly in size from species
to species. State and federal laws merely require that the *percentages by
weight* be given for each species in a mixture, and not the *relative numbers*
of each species per pound. Table 8-2 shows average number of seeds per
pound, and shows how seeding rates of individual species are adjusted to
compensate for varying seed size. The seeding rates are not directly pro-
portional, since the mortality of smaller seeds is greater than for larger
seeds in turf seeding.

Table 8-1
Seed Size and Planting Rates

Species	Seeds per Pound	Pounds/1,000 sq. ft.
Kentucky bluegrass	1,000,000 to 2,200,000	1 - 2
Red fescue	350,000 to 600,000	3 - 5
Perennial ryegrass	250,000	5 - 9
Tall fescue	170,000 to 220,000	5 - 9
Creeping bentgrass	5,000,000 to 7,000,000	0.5 - 1.5

Preparation of the Seedbed

It is important to improve the soil before planting because it is almost impossible to alter the soil after the grass is planted. Where needed, lime, organic matter, and fertilizers high in phosphate and potassium should be incorporated to depths of 6 to 8 inches before planting. The goal should be preparation of a seedbed that will have 6 to 8 inches of mellow soil through which roots will readily grow. The mature root system of healthy turfgrass should not be less than 6 inches, but most of that root system must be regenerated each year when growth begins after the cool dormant

Figure 8-3. After mixing fertilizer (and lime, if needed) with the topsoil, level the soil with a hand rake in preparation for seeding. (Courtesy, Danville Area Community College)

season. Place good topsoil to the depth of the expected root zone. The first step in building construction or landscaping should be the stockpiling of the valuable topsoil. After the construction is complete the topsoil can be spread over the seedbed to establish the new lawn.

The improvement of soil drainage may be an important requirement. If this is the case, the placement of plastic tile drains leading to suitable outlets should be done after the topsoil has been rough graded. Drains may be necessary on heavy-textured soils that drain slowly, or on sites with a high water table. Drains are sometimes needed to intercept and carry away waters coming from other areas. Drainage is relatively inexpensive when installed before planting, but correction of poor drainage on established turf is costly.

In the humid regions of the country (Figure 1-1), practically all soils are acid, varying only in degree. Lime may be incorporated to correct soil acidity to some depth and maintain a soil reaction favorable to grass root development. Such correction can be made over a period of years by topdressing turf with lime, but it is far more efficiently done by mixing lime throughout the intended root zone. Topsoil is always in scarce supply, and the turf manager may be faced with a need for improvement of subsoil or raw excavated soil material left at the surface. Fortunately, it may be

Figure 8-4. Making the final grade in preparation for seeding. (Courtesy, The Toro Company)

possible to improve this subsoil or raw material by the deep incorporation of lime (if the soil is acid), organic matter, and fertilizer through the intended root zone.

Adding Lime and Fertilizer

The amount of lime needed is readily determined by a soil test that can be made at any reliable soil-testing laboratory. Since grass roots prefer moderate to good fertility, the addition of a complete fertilizer high in phosphates and potassium should be made during seedbed preparation. To compensate for the lack of humus in subsoils and excavated materials, the addition of peat humus may be needed. A practical procedure is to apply all of the materials needed for improving the soil for the seedbed on the surface of the rough graded turf area. These materials may then all be mixed through the depth of soil being improved by using a rototiller. Tilling the seedbed, in several directions, will completely mix the soil amendments with the native soil. When mixing is completed, the soil will be quite loose and should be rolled to lightly compact the soil. It is then ready for final grading and the final surface treatments before seeding. In preparing the seedbed apply 50 pounds of ground limestone per 1,000

Figure 8-5. Seedbed preparation using a small powered tiller. (Courtesy, Fritz Bateman)

square feet of soil surface and 5 to 10 pounds of a 12-25-13 or similar starter fertilizer per 1,000 square feet of soil surface.

Propagation by Seed

In establishing turf from seed, four factors are necessary for seed germination: (1) live seed, (2) adequate moisture, (3) sufficient soil warmth, and (4) adequate aeration. If one or more of these factors are not present, the seed will not germinate or the plant will be too weak to survive.

Seeding

Take care not to plant the grass seed too deep in the soil. The smaller the size of the seeds, the greater is the necessity for shallow planting. Cover the larger ryegrass and fescue seeds to provide sufficient contact with moist soil to insure good germination. Very small seeds such as bentgrass require only partial covering for successful growth. Seeding rates may be better evaluated by considering the number of seeds spread per unit of soil surface. A good lawn can be established if 15 to 20 viable grass seeds are applied to each square inch of prepared soil surface. An easy way to check the seeding rate is by cutting a one inch square hole in a sheet of paper and

Figure 8-6. Seeding with a mechanical seeder. (Courtesy, South Side Country
Club)

Figure 8-7. Seeding with a slit seeder. (Courtesy, Danville Country Club)

then randomly dropping the paper on the seeded lawn area and counting the number of seeds in the cut out square. To insure uniform seed distribution, spread one-half of the allotted seed for a specific turf area in a north-south direction, and the remaining half over the same area in an east-west direction. The seed should then be raked-in lightly to provide shallow coverage without affecting the uniform distribution of the seed. Avoid raking the seed into ridges or windrows. Successful planters usually pull the rake through the soil in one direction only, as in combing hair, rather than pushing the rake back and forth in the soil. After seeding the area should be rolled lightly with a roller to firm the seed into the soil and then mulched with straw.

Mulching not only reduces the amount of soil crusting that will occur with rainfall or watering, but it also retards evaporation and helps to keep the soil moist enough to stimulate germination of the seed. Some grasses have long germination periods (bluegrass needs 14 to 21 days), and even the more rapidly germinating species will produce a more uniform stand when lightly mulched. If mulched evenly, without completely covering the soil, it is never necessary to remove the mulch that eventually decays in place. Apply one bale of straw per 1,000 square feet or for large areas one ton per acre. The mulch can be applied by hand on small lawn area or with a power mulch blower on larger areas.

Special Treatment on Slopes

On steep slopes it may be necessary to lay sod and stake or peg it in place until the sod has knitted down. On less difficult slopes, a strip of sod laid at the top of the slope and with additional strips placed at intervals of 10 feet or more in contours across the slope is adequate to stop washing so that intermediate areas may be seeded in the usual fashion. When slopes are less than 20 percent grade, use erosion control fabric to hold the seeds from washing. This fabric will not only prevents soil erosion, but will also aid in keeping the soil surface moist while protecting the young seedlings from undue exposure to the sun.

VEGETATIVE PLANTING OF NEW TURF

Several better grasses for turf in southern regions are reproduced vegetatively by planting pieces of stolons, commonly called stolonizing, or by plugging. These grasses include carpetgrass, centipedegrass, St. Augustinegrass, zoysia and the hybrid cultivars of bermudagrass. Soil preparation steps are the same for stolonizing and plugging as for seeding. When the final surface soil treatment of the intended lawn area has been completed, the area is then ready for planting.

Stolonizing

Freshly harvested sprigs should be planted as soon as possible after they are dug from the nursery. Sprigs must be kept cool and moist if planting is delayed. Normally 5 to 10 bushels of sprigs are required for each 1,000 square feet of lawn area. The sprigs are produced by cutting established sod of the desired grass, shaking out the soil, and then chopping the stolons into such lengths that each has two to four nodes. New shoots and roots develop at the nodes. In planting, at least one node must be below the ground surface to insure rooting, and one end of the sprig with leaves must be above ground so that top growth can resume. Spread the sprigs over the surface and then partially cover them with screened soil. The objective is to spread enough soil or compost to insure rooting, but not enough to cover all leaf tissue. After stolonizing is complete, irrigate the area to ensure good soil sprig contact.

Figure 8-8. Plugging—small plugs of sod are set at measured intervals.

Plugging

As with sprigging, preparation of the seedbed should be handled in the same manner as preparation for seeding. Sod is cut in a nursery 1 to 2 inches thick. A separate machine then cuts the harvested sod into individual 2 inch square plugs. The plugs are planted 6 to 12 inches on center in the prepared soil. In the North, zoysia can be planted into an existing bluegrass lawn using this technique to convert to an all zoysia lawn. Hand plungers are used to plant small lawn areas, but on golf course fairways, machines plant the plugs. Zoysia is most frequently established as turf using this method. If the plugs are set in moist soil, light watering after planting is sufficient. Weed control, either by hand or with herbicides, is very important during this establishment stage. Water the plugs, when necessary, to assure continued growth.

Sodding

There are often areas in the landscape where an "instant" lawn is required. These areas should be sodded with a mixture of grass varieties that will adapt to the climatic area. While speed of establishment is usually the reason for sodding, erosion control is also a valid reason to sod a lawn. Grass seed is planted in farm fields and allowed to grow one or two years and then harvested with a sod cutter. The pieces of sod are usually 12

Figure 8-9. A vegetative planting of zoysia—two months after planting
            small sprigs (upper), two months after planting with 2-inch
            blocks of sod (middle), and sod which is 18 months old
            (bottom). (*Alabama Agricultural Experiment Station Circ. 85*)

inches wide, 6 feet long, and 5/8 of an inch thick. After cutting, the sod is
rolled up similar to the way a sleeping bag is rolled. Each roll will contain
one square yard of sod. The steps in site preparation for sodding are the
same as in seeding a new lawn area. If possible the site should be watered
the night before the sod is laid. This will provide a better interface between
the existing soil and new sod. Some sod is being sold with the soil washed
off for use primarily on golf course greens where the new site soil may be
different from the soil where the sod was grown.

Figure 8-10. Rotary pop-up sprinklers operating on a golf course (top). Proper operation of a sprinkler system requires a skillful turf manager (bottom). (Courtesy, South Side Country Club)

CARE OF NEW PLANTINGS

Watering

Watering of new plantings is always necessary in the drier regions and is often important in humid regions to supplement rainfall. Drying out is quite harmful to germinating seed. A heavy soil crust may form and prevent sprouts from reaching the surface, thus killing the seedlings. Sprigs and sod pieces are not as sensitive to drying as young seedlings, but they also may suffer from drought. If possible, irrigation should be provided whenever rainfall is inadequate.

There are three sound rules for watering: (1) always use a fine mist-like spray rather than dumping large amounts of water in a heavy downpour; (2) do not add water faster than the soil will readily absorb it, but continue until the soil is well moistened to a depth of several inches; and (3) avoid waterlogging of the soil, particularly if water produces pools that are slow to drain. Waterlogged soil and surface pools of water invite turf diseases that are difficult to halt when once started. Damping-off of young seedlings may wipe out effected areas.

Mowing

Mow the new lawn when the seedlings are 25 percent taller than the height of cut. For example, mow the new lawn at 2 inches when the new seedlings are 2½ inches tall. Perhaps more important than when the first mowing should occur is the principle of using a very sharp mower blade for this first mowing. A dull blade will pull the new seedling from the soil instead of cutting them off. For areas seeded with a lawn mixture, mowing may begin when the rapidly growing grasses reach a height of more than 2 inches. However, it is very important to set the lawn mower to cut no closer than 1½ inches. The objective is to check the growth of the quick-growing species so they will not compete unduly with the slower-starting desirable permanent grasses. Cutting closer than ½ inch will damage the permanent grasses that need to make considerable top growth before tillering and the production of creeping stems begins.

Fertilizing the New Turf

Fertilizing the new turf should not be a problem if the seedbed was adequately fertilized before planting. If this is the case no fertilizing should

Figure 8-11. Care must be exercised when mowing new turf. (Courtesy, South Side Country Club)

be needed until the next normal fertilization period, either spring of fall. If the grass is growing slowly or yellow green in color a light fertilization may be necessary. The application of a 32-4-8 or similar fertilizer, with at least 50 percent of the nitrogen slowly available is advisable. Apply 3 pounds of this fertilizer per 1,000 square feet of lawn surface. Uniform and complete coverage of the area is essential since fertilizer will move downward into the soil, but not laterally. Areas on which no fertilizer falls will continue to starve, and areas that receive too much may be burned by the soluble fertilizer. Water in the fertilizer using a light spray and continue until the upper inch or two of soil is moistened.

EXPLANATION OF TECHNICAL TERMS

- **Germination** of seed is expressed in percentage of the *number of seed* in any lot that will produce sprouts and roots under laboratory conditions. It applies only to the seed of the grass. State regulations require all seed to carry a tag or label showing the percentage of germination and the date when tested.

- **Purity** of seed is based on the weight of the seed lot made up of the kind of seed offered for sale. Thus 75 percent purity of a particular lot of bluegrass seed would mean that 25 percent of each pound is made up of other kinds of grass seed other than the one on the label. All seed lots offered for sale must give the purity on the label. Purchasers should look for this information on all seed lots.

- **Mulching** is a term used to describe any surface covering on the soil. The following mulch materials can be used—straw, hay, or shavings. Mulches are useful on new grass planting to prevent puddling of soil from pounding rain and to reduce surface drying. Mulches on new grass seeding must not be so thick or dense as to prevent necessary light from reaching the germinating seedlings. Some turf managers use a coarse mulch immediately after seeding and then remove the excess with a fork when the seedlings reach the stage of needing more light.

- **Seedbed** is the prepared soil for new planting. It literally means the bed into which seed is placed for germination, but is extended to mean grounds that have been prepared for sprigging or sodding.

Chapter 9

REGULAR CARE OF TURF

STANDARD PRACTICES

The regular maintenance of turf is comparatively inexpensive and simple on areas where soil conditions are favorable and adapted grasses are present. A good turfgrass calls for certain standard practices, to take advantage of the season and normal growth cycle of grass. Grass growth will improve soil conditions through the yearly cycle of root growth. Grass can heal injuries and recover from adverse conditions. New roots replace old ones yearly, and there is a continuous reproduction of new stems and shoots during the growing season. Perennial grasses have the potential for regaining vigor after unfavorable conditions are corrected.

SEASONS FOR MOST EFFECTIVE TREATMENTS

It is not uncommon to find that turf management practices are either put into effect at an unfavorable season or are in themselves undesirable. Modification of these practices or substitution of more favorable treatments will frequently produce improved turf, with no extra labor and expense. The following treatments are intended for growing average turfgrass. Special problems of renovating damaged turf will be discussed in the following chapter. For convenience, the following management practices are presented in seasonal order, beginning with early spring.

Liming to Correct Soil Acidity

Acid soils are universal in humid regions, unless lime has been applied. Soil acidity is constantly developing because of the use of fertilizers, the leaching effect of rainfall, and the removal of grass clippings that contain substantial amounts of calcium drawn from the soil. It is a simple matter to offset these losses by regular applications of finely ground limestone.

Figure 9-1.   Trimmer/weeder for edging and for difficult locations; engine powered and flexible. (Courtesy, Danville Area Community College)

In all humid regions, a light application yearly or a heavier treatment every two years will be sufficient.

Although some grasses are more tolerant of soil acidity than others, the soil conditions are more favorable for all grasses when soil acidity is corrected. Lime for topdressing turf should be finely ground. Coarse-ground limestone, ground oystershells, and similar materials have good lime content but are too slowly available when applied to the surface of established turfgrass. Finely ground limestone sifts through grass to the soil surface where it can correct acidity. There is no danger of burning grass with limestone.

Soil Testing

To make certain that sufficient lime is being applied a soil test should be made. If lime is needed only to correct for the acidity produced each year, 25 pounds per 1,000 square feet annually or 50 pounds in alternate years will suffice. If needed to correct accumulated acidity, larger amounts of lime should be applied. Doubling these rates will progressively correct excess soil acidity. The application of more than 50 pounds annually will not greatly speed up correction of acidity because limestone dissolves at a slow rate.

Late winter or early spring is a satisfactory time for liming, although autumn is a favorable season if this is a period when the work schedule will permit it. There is no harm in applying lime at any season of the year; the sooner it is spread after the need is known, the better will be the effect. As with other materials, uniform spreading of lime over the soil surface is essential for good results.

Under no conditions should lime applications be regarded as a substitute for fertilization. Instead, it is a supplement to fertilizer and helps to balance the response from use of plant food. Lime frequently does aid in making turf more drought resistant and in reducing run-off losses of rain.

FERTILIZING ESTABLISHED TURF

Turfgrasses growing in the cooler regions need fertilizer applied four times each year. The best times are in early spring, late spring, early fall, and late fall. Turfgrasses will start growth two to three weeks earlier in the spring if fertilizer is applied in March or early April, depending on the latitude. Not only does early fertilization speed spring greenup but it also helps the cool-season grasses to heal injuries and thickens the turfgrass before summer annual weeds can invade the turf. Fertilization during May will provide the turfgrass the nutrients necessary to survive the hot summer growing season. A similar fertilization in late August or in September will stimulate the production of new tillers and rhizomes for the following year. This fertilization well also helps maintain a vigorous and green turf until late fall or early winter. A late fall application of fertilizer, especially nitrogen, will keep the root system growing until the ground freezes. This can also improve early spring greenup of the grass. Such a fertilization program provides the desired grasses the most benefit, and denies such benefits to the summer annual weeds.

For turf in warmer regions, make at least two applications of fertilizer; however, the timing should be adjusted. Make the first application in very early spring and again in midsummer when the first application is nearly exhausted. These grasses thrive in hot weather, and therefore are better able to compete with summer annual weeds if they are never short of nutrients.

Fertilizer Composition

Maintenance fertilizers should be high in nitrogen, but also have moderate amounts of phosphate and potash. To avoid undue stimulation immediately after fertilization and to assure a sustained flow of nutrients to the grass, at least half the nitrogen should be in a slowly available form. The exact analysis of the mixed fertilizer is not crucial; it may have a guaranteed analysis of 23-3-7, 32-4-8, or some similar content. Each will produce equal results if properly used.

Amount of Fertilizer

The amount of fertilizer should be adjusted to the native fertility of the soil, the length of the growing season, and the amount of foot traffic. Turfgrasses on soils of low fertility need more fertilizer. The longer the growing season, the greater the need is for fertilizer. In general the average application should be 1 pound of actual nitrogen per 1,000 square feet four times each year. Pounds of actual nitrogen are calculated by multiplying the pounds of fertilizer in the bag by the percentage of nitrogen shown on the fertilizer label. For example, a 50 pound bag of 32-4-8 fertilizer will contain 16 pounds of actual nitrogen (50 pounds × 32 percent). Apply a bag of 32-4-8 fertilizer on a 16,000 square foot lawn area. This rate is one pound of actual nitrogen per 1,000 square feet.

Figure 9-2.   Rotary spreader mounted on a golf cart, for rapid coverage of extensive areas.

Spreading Fertilizer

All fertilizers must be spread uniformly over the turfgrass surface since they do not move laterally in the soil. Failure to provide uniform distribution will produce a very irregular response of the grass; the strips or spots that are missed will get no benefit from the fertilizer. Uniform spreading is also desirable to avoiding over-stimulation of grass in some areas. Fertilizers should not burn the turfgrass if applied correctly. To aid in uniform spreading, fertilizer should be spread with a fertilizer spreader set to deliver the desired amount. There are two major types of fertilizer spreaders. The drop or gravity spreader will provide a very accurate application of fertilizer; however, the application will be very slow because the spreader will only cover a 24 inch wide strip. The rotary or cyclone spreader will cover a 6 to 12 foot wide strip and give a uniform application. These spreaders can quickly fertilize large turf areas.

ROLLING TURF AREAS

In the regions where considerable winter freezing and thawing of the soil occur, the turfgrass may appear rough in spring. There is a belief that spring rolling is necessary for a smooth turf. Use a light water-filled roller to "replant" the grass plants. Repeated rolling when the soil is wet and soggy, particularly with a heavy roller, causes undesirable compaction of heavy-textured soils. Since grass roots will penetrate only into soil layers that are well aerated, spring rolling may restrict the new roots to the uppermost layers of soil. It is this newly developing portion of the root system that will do most of the work of providing nutrients and water from the soil during the growing season. The freezing and thawing of heavy soils are effective natural means of producing a well-aerated soil, and unwise rolling in spring may nullify this influence. The objective in sound turf maintenance should be to roll sparingly, and thus take full advantage of soil freezing to produce soil structure favorable to grass roots. The roller should only be heavy enough to press the crowns of the grass plants into the soil and smooth the soil surface. Since the weight of the roller needed varies with the soil, a water ballast roller that permits weight adjustment is helpful. For most soil conditions, a hollow steel roller is heavy enough without any water ballast. Heavy spring rolling often retards grass growth for the entire season. Rolling is rarely, if ever, an important management practice in warmer regions where winter soil freezing is not common.

Rolling should not be done to correct an irregular surface due to worm casts, crawfish mounds, or similar elevations. A better treatment is to use the necessary chemicals to kill the pests, and use a scarifying machine set to knock down and distribute the mounds of earth without tearing up the grass. Rolling should not be done to smooth the soil surface at the time of planting or to correct marked irregularities in the surface due to rutting caused by heavy machine operation when the soil was soft. The best treatment is to fill the low spots with screened topsoil or compost, followed by dragging with a flexible steel mat, as is the practice on golf greens.

TOPDRESSING TURFGRASSES

This treatment is usually not necessary on homelawns. However, there are a few special situations where topdressing may be warranted.

- Where grass has been established on a very poor soil, topdressing with a loamy topsoil that has been screened to remove stone and trash may be useful. The topdressing may be applied in late spring or early fall when the grass is actively growing and will recover from the addition of the topdressing material. A thin layer of material, not to exceed 1/4 inch in depth at any one application, can be applied by machine or by hand using an aluminum scoop. The dressing should be worked-in promptly by dragging with a flexible steel mat made from a piece of chain link fence. Repeated topdressing at intervals of several weeks will gradually produce a smoother turfgrass.

- When the turf surface is very irregular because of irregular settling of the newly planted sod, the depressions may be filled after the planting is well established by one or more topdressings. The topdressing should be spread over the entire rough surface and worked into the low spots by repeated dragging with a flexible steel mat.

- Periodic topdressing can correct severe surface matting on turf with strong surface creeping stems, such as creeping bentgrass and St. Augustinegrass. For matted areas, first verticut the surface with a vertical mower to remove most of the matted stems and then apply topdressing. This appears drastic, but it is effective in reestablishing a well-rooted turfgrass. For creeping bentgrass, this treatment will yield the best results if done in early spring or early fall together with spring and fall core aerification. For warm-season grasses, it may be done any time during the growing season.

Figure 9-3. The above aerifier is used for golf course greens (top). Note the plugs after operation in the lower photo (bottom). (Courtesy, South Side Country Club)

AERIFYING TURF AREAS

Aerifying machines are used to temporally improve compact soil conditions and reduce thatch accumulation. The soil cores are usually ½ inch in diameter and the spacing of the tines on the aerifier will vary from 2 inches to 10 inches. The more holes made, the better the aerification job. Use machines that have closely spaced tines or go over the turf area several times. The best type of aerifier is one that removes a soil core to depths of 2 to 3 inches. After aerification, the soil cores left at the surface, can be broken up and spread over the surface by dragging with a flexible steel mat. This treatment, when needed, is most effective if done before applying fertilizer or lime. The holes produced by aerification permit deep penetration of fertilizers and lime.

MOWING

Improper mowing does more damage to home lawns than any other maintenance practice. Homeowners usually set their mowers to cut the grass so short that the grass is given a setback with each mowing. Most home lawns will tolerate regular mowing at a height of 2 inches, but they will do better if cut at a height of 3 inches. Cutting grass shorter than these lengths may gradually weaken the turfgrass by repeatedly defoliating the plants. Since all of the food used by plants for growth is manufactured in the leaves, excessive removal of leaves prevents food-making and weakens the plant. When repeated, excessively close mowing gradually exhausts the food reserves to the point where the plant loses its ability to endure drought, heat, disease pressure, and competition with aggressive weeds.

Excessively close mowing in spring is particularly harmful, since reduced food-making depresses development of the spring crop of new roots. The shallow root system that results from close cutting in spring will weaken the grass for the entire growing season.

The objective in mowing grass is to cut periodically at heights that will stimulate a more prostrate type of growth, without weakening the grass. Only the grasses that can respond to such cutting, are useful for fine turf. A few grasses will tolerate very close mowing when accompanied by special care and these are used on golf putting greens. Home lawns are different from putting greens, and any attempt to produce turf similar to golf greens merely by closer cutting is disastrous since it works against normal growth processes.

Figure 9-4. This golf course greens mower (top) is designed for very close cutting. A triplex greens mower (bottom) for rapid, precise maintenance. (Courtesy, South Side Country Club)

Figure 9-5.   A lightweight fairway mower. (Courtesy, Danville Country Club)

Figure 9-6.   This mower is able to turn sharply on lawn areas. (Courtesy, M.
            Thomas)

Height of Cutting

Lawn mowers used for home lawns should be set to cut 2½ to 3 inches in height. Permitting the grass to grow taller than this induces a stemmy erect habit of growth rather than the desired dense prostrate growth habit. The frequency of mowing should be such as to keep grass from exceeding 3½ inches in height. In periods of rapid growth, mowing may be needed twice a week; at other times, once a week may be sufficient. In cooler periods and in dry seasons, frequency of mowing may be once in two or more weeks. Under no condition should the grass produce seed heads, since this will exhaust the food reserves and retard leaf and shoot development for a considerable period.

Turf areas should be mowed into the fall as long as they continue growth. Permitting a long growth in fall merely encourages an increase in disease development.

Figure 9-7. A rotary riding mower for lawns and parks.

Adjusting the Mower

Height of cut is crucial, therefore, the lawn mower should be carefully set to cut to the desired height. Adjustment of the mower is simple and easy. There are two principal types of lawn mowers—those with rotary horizontal blades and the reel type. The adjustment of rotary mowers is accomplished by devices to raise or lower the wheels. Place the mower on a level floor or sidewalk, and measure the height of the cutting blade from the floor. Raise or lower the wheel setting until the desired height is achieved. Make certain that all wheels have the same setting. Remember that cutting turfgrass a little long does no damage, but cutting it too short may seriously weaken the grass. Reel-type mowers are used on golf course greens, tees, and fairways, but seldom on home lawns. Reel mower cutting height adjustments are usually done by setting the height of the front roller. Check the owner's manual for individual mower adjustment procedures.

Figure 9-8. A walk-behind 48-inch mower is widely used in commercial operations.

Removal of Clippings

When the amount of clippings produced by mowing the grass is such that they do not readily sift down into the turf, it is best to remove them. Such clippings are not only unsightly, but their continued presence on top of the grass is an invitation to diseases that prefer the higher humidity under the mat of clippings. If clippings are heavy enough to require removal, this should be done promptly before fungus diseases have an opportunity to develop. The clippings that sift down through the grass to the soil are

Figure 9-9. This lawn tractor is equipped with an optional power bagger to remove clippings. (Courtesy, M. Thomas)

helpful since they add to its fertility. Grass clippings will decompose rapidly and do not contribute to thatch build up.

WATERING TURF

In all regions with less than about 40 inches of annual rainfall, irrigation is essential for good turf maintenance. For humid regions, irrigation is desirable during periods of prolonged drought. The turf manager should install an inexpensive rain gauge to keep track of rainfall. Such gauges should be set on a post in the open, and read each time there is an appreciable amount of rain. By keeping a record of rainfall, the manager can easily figure out the need for watering. Whenever a period of 7 to 10 days elapses with less than an inch of recorded rainfall, the soil moisture is being exhausted to the point where grass will wilt in midday.

The capacity of the soil to store water for plant use depends on its structure and the ease with which water enters the soil. Thin turf on soils that cake and crust easily may lose much of the rainfall as runoff. Soils that produce strong turfgrass plants usually provide good rooting depth and a rapid water infiltration rate. Turfgrasses are rather tolerant of short dry periods, and renew growth promptly after being wilted. Thus, there is no need for alarm if short droughts occur.

Figure 9-10.   All sprinklers should be located and adjusted as needed to
provide uniform coverage of the turf. (Courtesy, L. R.
Nelson Manufacturing Co.)

Watering is not a substitute for proper fertilization or good mowing practices. A well-managed turf will need less supplemental watering if the management practices encourage strong turfgrass growth. Heavy watering, which is so often practiced on turf with automatic sprinkler systems, compacts the soil and tends to cause waterlogged soil on all but sandy soils. Roots are unable to survive on waterlogged soils because of poor aeration, and this makes the turfgrass less able to endure limited rainfall. Also, over watering in warm weather induces leaf diseases and benefits weeds, such as crabgrass, which thrive in summer heat. Water should be added only when needed. Periodic probing of soil with a screw driver or soil auger to determine how moist the soil is in the upper six inches is a useful supplement to rain gauge readings.

Frequent light sprinklings in hot weather benefit summer weeds more than the turfgrasses, particularly if the soil is only superficially moistened. As a rule, water to wet each area to a depth of about six inches, moving the sprinkler from area to area as the watering system permits. This is about one inch of water applied to the soil surface and will take the homeowner about one hour to apply. Water the lawn deeply but less frequently for best results. Normally one such watering per week will suffice except on the droughty kinds of soils or where much of the water runs off. Watering should cease whenever rainfall provides enough moisture,

Figure 9-11. A well-designed automatic sprinkler system is designed to give complete coverage. (Courtesy, The Toro Company)

and be resumed only when the soil is again approaching dryness in the root zone.

The time of day for watering is not important except that it should be completed early enough so that the grass leaves are dry by nightfall. When grass goes into the night with wet leaves, the situation is ideal for development of leaf diseases. The claim that watering in the sun will scald grass leaves is not valid. Any such scalding is probably caused by waterlogging of the soil and the resulting death of roots where drainage is inadequate.

Turfgrass growing on very sandy soils, or on infertile soils with low humus content, will need more attention to maintain adequate moisture than grass on better soils. Under extreme conditions, it may be necessary to remove the sod, improve soil conditions to a depth of several inches, and then replace the sod.

Steep and sloping terraces frequently suffer from moisture stress even when rainfall appears adequate. Both rainfall and irrigation water tend to run off the slopes. Water must be applied slowly on such locations to permit absorption by the turfgrass. The top of the slope will require more watering than the bottom, because water responds to gravity and moves downhill. The watering of slopes to moisten the soil to the desired root depth requires more time and attention than level areas. Examine the soil with a trowel to make sure the water is actually moistening the soil.

Figure 9-12. Thin-and-thatch machine. Useful for thinning surface mats of sodbound turf; for suppressing bermudagrass in the transition zone (see Figure 1-1); and for removing crabgrass, in preparation for fall seeding of cool season grasses.

EXPLANATION OF TECHNICAL TERMS

- **Calibration** refers to the process of adjusting a fertilizer spreader and measuring the output until the delivery of materials reaches the desired rate. Different materials flow at different rates and sometimes different lots of the same material flow at different rates. It is wise, to calibrate spreaders for spreading seed, fertilizer, pesticides, or soil amendments just before making applications.

- **Thatching machines** may be one of several types that scratch the turfgrass or make slits or incisions into the turf. These include slicing machines, verticut machines, thatchers, and spikers. The important factor is to choose the machine best suited to the job of breaking through the surface crust.

- **Soil testing** is a term used to describe a method of taking representative soil samples and having these tested for acidity (or alkalinity), available phosphorus and potash. Sometimes, the available supplies of soil calcium and magnesium are measured. Soil test results are usually interpreted in terms of the amounts of specific materials that should be added to make the soil suitable for turf growth.

- **Topdressing** is any material or mixture applied as a surface dressing to turf. The better types of mixed topdressings are made of fairly fertile topsoil blended with sand and organic matter. Commercially prepared topdressings are available in some sections of the country. On the other hand, so-called topdressing is often nothing more than screened soil of uncertain quality.

Chapter 10

CONTROLLING WEEDS IN TURF

WEED CONTROL STRATEGY

A good weed control strategy consists of exploiting opportunities in the following ways: (1) making conditions more favorable for the desired grasses and less favorable for weed growth, thus invoking the principles of natural competition; (2) reducing the opportunities for the introduction of weed seed by using weed-free grass seed mixtures and preventing weed seed production in the turf; and (3) attacking weeds with herbicides at growth stages when the weeds are most vulnerable. From this general plan, it should be obvious that the use of herbicides without taking care of other

Figure 10-1. Two types of hand sprayers for application of liquids. (Courtesy, Fritz Bateman)

factors is not an adequate method of weed control. When used as the principal or only weapon, the beneficial results from herbicides are temporary and the desired improvement in the quality of the turf is not achieved.

An abundance of weeds in a turf area is evidence that conditions are not satisfactory for good turfgrass growth. Nature's own method of controlling certain types of vegetation is to provide such stiff competition by the desired plants that the undesirable kinds of plants tend to be crowded out. A healthy turf—composed of well-adapted grasses and properly managed—will make such a dense cover that weeds will have difficulty in gaining a foothold.

MANAGEMENT FACTORS

The following are some factors that the turf manager should review before starting a program of weed control. Consider the following questions.

- Does the turf area now contain the grass varieties that are suited to the particular climatic area?

- Are the best grass varieties for the intended use of the turfgrass growing on the site?

- Does the soil pH, soil drainage, and/or soil permeability seriously depresses grass vigor?

- Does the schedule of fertilizing provide a continuing supply of nutrients at seasons when the desired grass derives the greatest benefits?

- Are the mowing schedule and height of cut favorable for the growth of desired grasses?

- Is shading by trees limiting the turfgrass growth?

- Does the watering schedule provide enough moisture to prevent grass wilting?

- Have grass diseases or insects weakened the grass, and thus provided easy entry and competition from weeds?

The turf manager should decide which of these are important, and set some priorities about which factors need attention. This brain work is inexpensive and not physically exhausting, but may suggest the tactics that will give the most rewarding results. Each of these factors is discussed in other chapters of this book.

KEEPING OUT WEED SEEDS

Weak, open turf offers an excellent opportunity for introduction of more weeds by seedling establishment. Most weeds are aggressive because of their ability to establish seedlings and make persistent growth under conditions less favorable for turfgrasses. Most of the troublesome weeds produce great numbers of seeds, and the distribution of weed seed by wind, water and animals are remarkably ingenious. However, the establishment of new plants from seed is the weakest and most vulnerable point of the weed life cycle. Annual weeds in particular must reproduce by seeds yearly so that measures to prevent seed formation, eliminate the entrance of new seed, or discourage the growth of young weed seedlings can be very effective means of control. Besides production and spread of weed seeds from weeds already established in the turf, the manager should guard against planting weed seeds that may be in cheap grass seed mixtures. State and federal laws require that weed seed be reported on labels of all seed packages; read the label!

MOWING PRACTICES

Mowing practices can be adjusted so that some weed species are largely

Figure 10-2. **Mowing practices can be adjusted so that some weed species are largely prevented from producing seed. (Courtesy, Danville Country Club)**

prevented from producing seed; this combined with timely use of herbicides will constitute good weed control practice. Mowing home lawns too short is a major reason for weedy turf. Most home lawns will have fewer weeds if the height of cut is raised to 3 inches instead of the usual 1½ or 2 inches. Taller grass can better compete with weeds for water and nutrients. Mow tall should be the rule, not the exception, for turfgrass.

SOIL AS A SOURCE OF WEED SEEDS

Weed seeds are very persistent in soil. Only a part of the seeds that matured in a single season will germinate promptly. Some seeds will lay dormant for many seasons before germinating, and thus, the campaign against weeds must be sustained. However, if new additions of weed seed are prevented, then the control measures become progressively more effective each year.

WEED CONTROL WITH HERBICIDES

The pesticide industry has been successful in developing herbicides that are selective in their action; that is, they kill or inhibit specific weeds without seriously retarding the growth of desirable turfgrass. The following precautions should be observed in the use of herbicides:

- **Select the herbicide**—Read the manufacturer's label and accompanying printed instructions as to the kinds of weeds that the herbicide will control, how to use it, and any special precautions. Herbicides are powerful compounds and may cause damage if improperly used.

- **Conditions for treatment**—Treat turfgrass areas with herbicides when soil moisture is good and the weeds are making good growth. The weeds are most vulnerable under those conditions. An exception to this general rule is the use of preemergence herbicides, as for crabgrass control, to prevent the germination of weed seeds.

- **Always follow printed precautions**—The turf manager should take appropriate care to see that sprays do not drift onto other vegetation such as flowers, shrubs, trees, and vegetables. Read the precautions on the herbicide package, and protect susceptible plants.

- **Do not treat seedling grasses**—Seedling grasses are far more sensitive to herbicides than are more mature plants. It is important to apply herbicides well before any reseeding of grass so the herbicide may be dissipated before planting grass seed. The time required to dissipate the herbicide is different for different chemicals. Read the label!

- **Herbicide-fertilizer mixtures**—Today many herbicides are mixed with turf fertilizers to make their application easy. Herbicides mixed with fertilizers may need to be applied to moist leaves to stick the herbicide on the weed leaf. Read and follow label directions.

- **Wait for treatments to become effective**—After treatment at the prescribed dosage of the herbicide, injury to the weeds may take from 3 to 10 days to become evident. Do not retreat in the mistaken idea that the treatment was not effective. Over-treatment is dangerous.

- **Follow recommendations**—The pesticide manufactures have figured out the most effective rates of application and the correct time of the year to apply the herbicide. They will also give precautions that must be followed to protect the environment. It is in violation of federal law to use a pesticide in a way not indicated on the label. Read the label, read it again, and *then* use the pesticide according to label directions.

For convenience, the weeds with similar growth characteristics and herbicide susceptibilities are grouped together in this discussion. They may not occur in such combinations in turf areas, but the treatments are recommended based on the presence of one or more of these weeds.

CONTROLLING SUMMER ANNUAL GRASSY WEEDS

Summer annual grass weeds

Crabgrass	Green foxtail
Small crabgrass	Yellow foxtail
Goosegrass (silver crabgrass)	Barnyard grass
Spreading witchgrass	

Summer annual grassy weeds are among the more troublesome pests in turf. Crabgrass is such an aggressive and widely occurring turf pest that special attention is warranted to cope successfully with it. These summer annuals must start from seeds that germinate after the onset of warm weather. The weed seedlings are not tolerant of shade, from tall growing turfgrasses. Where turf is thin, open, or weak, the seedlings rapidly become established and go on to crowd out the lawn species with their creeping stems and aggressive root systems. Crabgrass plants resemble turfgrasses in early growth stages. After midsummer, each creeping stem produces an upright shoot with seed stalks divided into three to six finger-like branches.

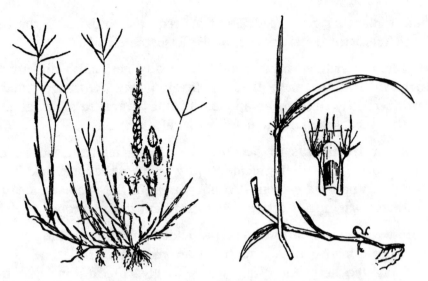

Figure 10-3.   Small crabgrass—this species has the same growth habit as the
larger species but the leaf blades and sheaths are not hairy.
(*U.S. Dept. of Agriculture Bulletins 123 and 461*)

Seed is produced in abundance, and falls to the ground where it remains dormant until the following spring and early summer. These grassy annual weeds cease active growth as fall approaches, and are killed by the first frost.

The weak point in the life cycle of these summer annual grassy weeds is at the time of seed germination when tender seedlings must become established. The time between onset of cool fall weather and the following spring is the time to stimulate permanent grasses to develop a dense turf that offers scant opportunity for annual seedlings to develop. In the cooler regions, fall renovation and fertilization at the close of the crabgrass growing season is a very effective management practice. Early spring fertilization and taller height of cut throughout the spring and summer can smother out the young weed seedlings.

In the warmer regions, greater reliance should be placed on very early fertilization to stimulate lawn grasses to make growth several weeks before annual grassy weeds germinate. Longer height of cut, particularly in the early part of the growing season, is quite effective in retarding or preventing establishment of the weed seedlings. Don't fertilize in the summer but just ahead of frost in the fall.

It should be clear that these management practices are important adjuncts to chemical control of crabgrass and other summer annual grasses. It is particularly important to water only occasionally, but deeply, to meet

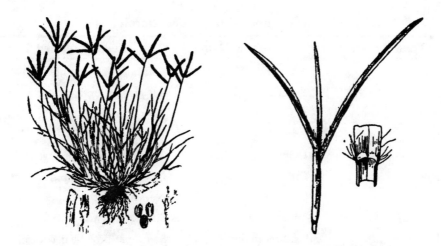

Figure 10-4. **Goosegrass—somewhat coarse and with a rosette of flattened stems under cutting.** (*U.S. Dept. of Agriculture Bulletins 123 and 461*)

the needs of the perennial grasses. Shallow, frequent watering is ideal for these grassy weeds and does little or nothing for permanent grass; therefore, the natural competition is shifted in favor of the weeds.

Chemical control is of two types—*preemergence* and *postemergence*. The preemergence herbicides are applied before the weed seeds germinate; whereas, the postemergence herbicides will be applied to the weed after it germinates.

- Table 10-1 shows preemergence grass weed herbicides; however, some have additional properties such as postemergence control or preemergence broadleaf weed control. Apply these herbicides two weeks before crabgrass seed germination is expected. Read and follow all label directions.

- Table 10-2 lists postemergence grass weed control herbicides; however, some have additional properties such as preemergence control. Most herbicides used on southern turfgrass should not be applied to northern turfgrass. Read and follow label directions.

With these herbicides it is essential to apply them in the amounts and in the manner specified by the manufacturer. These are plant killers and overdoses could be very damaging to desirable turf, especially weakened turf.

The other annual grassy weeds, goosegrass, spreading witchgrass, green and yellow foxtail, and barnyardgrass, are effectively controlled by applications of the same herbicides that are used to control crabgrass. Extra care

Table 10-1
Preemergence Grass Weed Herbicides

Trade Name	Common Name	Recommended Use
Aatrex	Atrazine	Southern lawns only
Balan	Benefin	All grasses except bent
Barricade	Prodiamine	New compound pre-broadleaf
Betasan	Bensulide	All grass varieties
Dacthal	DCPA	May need two applications
Dimension	Dithiopyr	New compound pre/post action
Gallery	Isoxaben	New also pre-broadleaf control
Image	Imazaquin	Southern lawns only
Pre-M	Pendimethalin	Some pre-broadleaf control
Princep	Simazine	Southern lawns only
Ronstar	Oxidiazon	Very good on goosegrass
Team	Trifluralin + Benefin	Northern lawns
Tupersan	Siduron	Can use after new lawn seeding

Table 10-2
Postemergence Grass Weed Herbicides

Trade Name	Common Name	Recommended Use
AAtrex	Atrazine	Southern lawns only
Acclaim	Penoxyprop-ethyl	Crabgrass
Dimension	Dithiopyr	Also some preemergent control
Impac	Quinclorac	Southern lawns only
MSMA	MSMA	Organic arsenicals
Poast	Sethoxydim	Southern lawns only
Princep	Simazine	Southern lawns only
Roundup	Glyphosate	Non-selective
Sencor	Metribuzin	Southern lawns only

must be exercised when using Roundup (non-selective) herbicide as it can kill any plant that it is sprayed on.

CONTROLLING GRASSY PERENNIALS

Grassy perennials are a very difficult group of turf weeds to control since they resemble turfgrasses in their tolerance of herbicide chemicals. Weedy species such as nimblewill (*Muhlenbergia schreberi*), quackgrass (*Agropyron repens*), switchgrass (*Panicum virgatum*), tall fescue (*Festuca arundinacea*), and yellow nutsedge will usually tolerate the close mowing of desirable turfgrass and may persist indefinitely in the lawn. Since they have a different foliage color and texture than the desirable turfgrass, they are objectionable in appearance. These perennial grass weeds can be controlled with a spot application of gylocate when they are actively growing. Gylocate will kill all green plant tissue that it is sprayed on so care must be exercised when applying it.

The following are specific control measures for some perennial grass weeds.

Figure 10-5. Three species of foxtail grasses that invade turf as summer annuals. (*U.S. Dept. of Agriculture Bulletin 123*)

- **Nutgrass or yellow nut sedge**—This is the common name given to several species of sedge that spread extensively by small nut-like tubers produced 1 to 4 inches below the ground surface. New infestations often occur in resodding jobs, where the sedge is introduced in the sod but not noticed when closely mowed. Nutgrass is not a grass, but has leaves that appear grasslike. All sedges have three-sided stems that serve as convenient identification characters. Yellow nut sedge plants like plenty of soil moisture thus are usually found in poorly drained lawn areas.

    MSMA has been applied for many years as an over the top herbicide to control nutsedge. Basagran also can be applied over-the-top to control nutgrass. Apply these herbicides in late May after the nutgrass has started its new growth. It is best to make the application a day or two after mowing when the nutgrass has begun to make new growth. In about one week, the weed will begin to sicken and die. However, repeated

Figure 10-6. Nutgrass—a grass-like pest in turf that persists and spreads by means of underground stems and nut-like tubers. (*U.S. Dept. of Agriculture Bulletin 123*)

treatments may be necessary to kill new sprouts produced by the previously dormant nuts in the soil. Applications spaced three to four weeks apart will kill successive crops of nutgrass, thus resulting in complete eradication. Some yellowing of desirable turf may occur after treatment, but usually there will not be any permanent damage done. Good mowing, watering, and fertilization practices will help minimize any damage to the desirable turf.

- **Tall fescue**—When grown under a monostand, tall fescue can be an acceptable lawn. However, when a bluegrass lawn has several tall fescue plants growing per square yard, the tall fescue is now called a weed. Many homeowners have tried digging up the weeds, but they always return. Spot treatment with Roundup is a very popular control technique for the homeowner. For the professional turf manager a new herbicide from LESCO called TFC (Tall Fescue Control) can be spot applied over the top to the tall fescue plants without damaging the existing desirable turfgrass.

- **Annual bluegrass** (*Poa annua*)—This has long been a major weed on golf courses but not a serious problem on homelawns. Annual bluegrass, commonly called poa, has three serious problems that cause turf managers to consider it a nasty weed. Poa leaves are a lighter green than bentgrass, thus, golf greens with patches of poa look mottled. In the late spring poa produces many flowers and seed heads that are white in color and destroy overall uniformity of the turf. Finally, and perhaps the most serious problem, poa is unavailable to survive hot weather. In July and August large areas of poa will "die" or go dormant leaving the golf course looking like a war zone. The following cultural practices can help to suppress the poa growth. Apply fertilizers that are low in phosphorus as poa is a heavy phosphorus user. Irrigate only when necessary and don't over water the turf, as poa can tolerate water-logged soil conditions better than bentgrass or bluegrass. Core aerify to eliminate compact soil conditions because poa roots grow better in compact soil than bluegrass or bentgrass roots. The use of light-weight mowing units with baskets to collect clippings has helped reduce the poa seeds dropping to the soil surface and the light-weight units tend to reduce the soil compaction problems that came from using old, heavy mowing equipment. Calcium and lead arsenate herbicides were applied in the 1950s and 1960s to suppress poa growth, but they are no longer available to the turf manager. The herbicide Ronstar can be applied to help control poa seed germination, but it will not control existing poa. Prograss herbicide has been used to gradually reduce poa populations while allowing the bentgrass

Figure 10-7. Nimblewill—a perennial grass difficult to control but susceptible to herbicides at the seeding stage. (*U.S. Dept. of Agriculture Bulletins 123 and 461*)

population to increase. However, this program will take several years to convert golf course greens and fairways from poa to bent or bluegrass.

- **Nimblewill**—This weed can be controlled with spot applications of Roundup during the late spring or summer, after it starts new growth.

CONTROLLING BROADLEAF WEEDS

Broadleaf weeds have leaves that are wide (not long and narrow as grass leaves), two seed cotyledons, and a netted or branched vein pattern. It is important to understand their life cycle to select the best control techniques and correctly time herbicide applications. Some of these weeds grow as summer annuals in the cooler northern United States while they

Figure 10-8. Nine common broadleaf weeds (knotweed, A; spotted spurge, B; lawn pennywort, C; buckhorn plantain, D; broadleaf plantain, E; dandelion, F; mouse-ear chickweed, G; common chickweed, H; henbit, I). (Courtesy, Amchem Products, Inc.)

may have more of a perennial growth habit in the South. In the past most broadleaf weeds were controlled with postemergence herbicides. Today new preemergence herbicides are available to prevent broadleaf weed seeds from germinating and infesting turfgrass.

Annual Broadleaf Weeds

Annual plants only live one growing season, produce a new crop of seeds, and then die. Annual broadleaf weeds can be divided into two smaller groups, summer annuals and winter annuals. The largest group, summer annuals, germinate each spring, grow and flower during the summer, and then die in that fall. The winter annuals germinate in the fall, go into dormancy during the winter, start growth again the following spring, produce seeds, and die that summer.

Broadleaf Weeds

Summer Annual Weeds	Winter Annual Weeds
Knotweed	Henbit
Lambsquarter	Common chickweed
Purslane	Mouse-ear chickweed
Spurge	
Yellow woodsorrel	

Chemical Control of Summer Annual Broadleaf Weeds

Control broadleaf summer annuals with a two or three-way herbicide mix applied in late May after weed germination. Prevent weed seed germination with a preemergence herbicide application made in early spring. A complete list of broadleaf herbicides is given later in this chapter.

Chemical Control of Winter Annual Broadleaf Weeds

Control broadleaf winter annuals with a two or three-way herbicide mix applied in late October after weed germination or in the early spring. Prevent the seeds from germinating with a preemergence herbicide application made in late summer. A complete list of broadleaf herbicides is given later in this chapter.

Perennial Broadleaf Weeds

Perennial weed seeds can germinate any time of the year. Perennial plants produce a new seed crop each year and continue to grow year after year and produce more seeds each year. The perennial broadleaf leaf weed group is considered a major lawn weed group. These weeds are best controlled with a postemergence herbicide. For identification purposes it will help to divide these weeds into subgroups by their growth habit. Rosette type weeds have their leaves in a circle around a very short stem; dandelion is the most common rosette type weed. Creeping lawn weeds spread by underground or above ground stems; creeping charlie is a very common creeping lawn weed. Broadleaf weeds that do not fit into either of the above two groups are then classed as upright lawn weeds.

Rosette type	Creeping or prostrate
Dandelion	Bindweed
Buckhorn plantain	Chinquefoil
Broadleaf plantain	Ground ivy
Thistles	Pennywort
Chicory	Speedwell
Curry dock	Yarrow

Upright non-creeping

Black medic
Red sorrel
White clover
Wild violet
Yellow rocket

Perennial broadleaf weeds have been controlled with 2,4-D or related compounds since the early 1950s. Several applications, 10 days to 2 weeks apart, may be necessary to control the more difficult weeds. Fortunately, most of these broadleaf weeds are easily controlled with a single application of a two or three-way mix of 2,4-D, MCPP, and/or dicamba. In recent years, two new postemergence herbicides, Turflon and Confront, have been sold that do not contain any 2,4-D or related compounds. It is essential to prevent any herbicide spray drift from contacting flowers, shrubs, trees, or vegetable plants as these herbicides can kill non-target plants. Treated weeds should begin to exhibit malformed growth in seven days, and after that the plants progressively decline. Some of these broadleaf weeds are more difficult to kill than others, and a second treatment about a month after the first may be necessary to completely kill the weeds. In the northern

Figure 10-9. Red sorrel—a perennial persistent weed that should be eradicated promptly since it spreads throughout turf areas when introduced. (*U.S. Dept. of Agriculture Bulletin 123*)

United States a late spring and an early fall postemergence herbicide application will ensure a season-long weed-free turf. In all treatments, it is essential to have the herbicide coat the leaves of the weeds. These pesticides are absorbed into the leaf tissue and moved inside the plant to kill the entire plant. Application is usually done by mixing the herbicides with water and spraying them on the entire lawn. Granular herbicides are usually combined with a fertilizer and applied with a fertilizer spreader to the entire lawn surface. Apply these products to wet grass foliage to stick the herbicide granules to the weed leaf. Do not treat newly planted turf areas until the grass seedlings are well established and making mature-type leaves, usually six weeks after germination. The dosage should be no greater than recommended for the particular formulation of the herbicide to protect the grass from damage.

Table 10-3 lists both preemergence and postemergence broadleaf weed control herbicides. Always read and follow label directions.

Table 10-3
Broadleaf Weed Control Herbicides

Trade Name	Common Name	Recommended Use
2,4-D	2,4-D	Popular in lawn care business
Barricade	Prodiamine	New preemergence herbicide
Banvel	Dicamba	Used in 2 or 3 way mixture
Contront	Triclopyr + Clopyralid	Popular in lawn care business
Gallery	Isoxben	New preemergence herbicide
MCPP	Mecoprop	Good clover control
Turflon	Triclopyr	May be mixed with Clopyralid

PRECAUTIONS TO TAKE WHEN USING HERBICIDES

All herbicides are powerful chemicals that are capable of causing injury to man and animals. Store and handle them so they will never contaminate food or feed. Keep out of the reach of children and away from animals. When using or handling herbicides, wear clean, dry clothes; avoid prolonged contact with the skin and wash promptly with soap after use; avoid inhalation of dusts or mists by using a mask completely covering the mouth and nose. Do not eat, drink or smoke until after washing your hands. To protect water resources, fish and wildlife, other vegetation, and animals, avoid contamination of lakes, streams and ponds. Insure that treatments are restricted to the target areas containing unwanted weeds.

Although moss and algae do not compete with grass for light, water, and nutrients nor do they attack grass as would a parasite of some sort, they are a clear indication of unsatisfactory growing conditions for grass. They are associated with low soil fertility, poor drainage, high soil acidity, improper watering, excessive shade, soil compaction, or any combination of these. To dispose of moss and algae in preparation for renovation, spray with a solution of copper sulfate made by dissolving five ounces of copper sulfate in four gallons of water. This quantity is sufficient for treating 1,000 square feet of surface. When the moss and algae have been killed, correct the basic conditions that caused these growths and reseed the area. As a part of preparation for reseeding, an application of 50 pounds of finely ground limestone per 1,000 square feet of ground surface should be made to inactivate the copper sulfate so that it will not be toxic to grass seedlings.

Figure 10-10. Self-propelled sprayer for rapid coverage of large turf areas (bottom) and computer control panel (top). (Courtesy, Danville Country Club)

Figure 10-11. The latest in self-
              contained storage
              facilities for chemicals.

Figure 10-12. Chemicals must be carefully used to prevent injury to people, domestic animals, and desirable kinds of wildlife. (Courtesy, Terra International, Inc., Professional Products)

EXPLANATION OF TECHNICAL TERMS

- **Selective herbicides** are pesticides that are capable of killing some types of plants but leaving other types uninjured. It is important to select a herbicide carefully. The labels on containers of herbicides will give detailed information. Read them!

- **Life cycle** is a term most frequently used in turf management when discussing weeds or other undesirable kinds of plants. The cycle consists of germination, seedling establishment, vegetative growth, seed formation, and death of the plant. A knowledge of the life cycle of a plant species is helpful in finding out how to suppress it.

- **Postemergence herbicides** are applied after the weed seeds germinate. See a weed, spray it.

- **Preemergence herbicides** prevent seed germination. They must be applied to the soil before weed seeds are expected to germinate.

- **Trade names** are those used by manufacturers and vendors of chemicals to identify the formulations that the particular company has to offer. Although the essential active chemical may be the same in several brands or named products, each named formulation may differ in strength, degree of solubility, fineness of granulation, combination with other chemicals, and purity. The label on all trade named products always gives detailed information on the active substance contained, and how best to use the product.

- **Common names** are those agreed upon by all parties concerned with the chemical industry as to the accepted name for the active substance. Thus, Benefin and Dicamba are common chemical names.

Chapter 11

CONTROLLING INSECTS AND OTHER TURF PESTS

Insects and other pests that infest turf may damage the grass, produce unsightly conditions, or be obnoxious because they attack or annoy people. Grubs, cutworms, and chinch bugs are examples of insects that seriously damage turf. Earthworms and ants are objectionable because the mounds or casts they create mar the turf surface. Chiggers, ticks, bees, wasps, and yellow jackets attack people but do little or no injury to the grass. Although sound turf management practices minimize the damage done by disease organisms, such practices are not always as effective in controlling insect pests. Healthy turf may endure heavy infestations of some insects without visible damage, while weak turf may be injured or even killed by the same populations. For example, 8 to 10 white grubs per square foot can kill weak

Figure 11-1. Rapid coverage of very large areas for control of insects or weeds. (Courtesy, Terra International, Inc., Professional Products)

turf; two to three times this number of grubs can live and eat grass roots, without serious injury to the grass, on vigorous turf with a strong root system. Proper fertilization, mowing at suitable height of cut, sound watering practices, and other good management practices are a vital part of the program of fighting insect pests.

For all types of turf-infesting insects, the first step in instituting control measures is to figure out the type of insect to be controlled. The following insect groups are described as an aid in identifying the true culprits and invoking the most appropriate weapons for control.

INSECTS THAT DAMAGE GRASS

- **Grubs**—These pests feed on the roots of grass. Grubs are the larval stage of a variety of beetles such as the May and June beetles, Japanese beetle, Asiatic garden beetle, Oriental beetle, several species of chafers, and the green June beetle. Most of these beetles have an annual life cycle in which eggs are laid by the adult beetles in green grass in summer. These eggs hatch in late July or early August into tiny grubs that feed on grass roots. The grubs may be found in infested turf during late summer and autumn. The turf manager must closely examine the top ½ to 1 inch of soil to find a grub infestation. The grubs are usually found in a curled or *C* position. They have white bodies with colored heads, and the hind part of the body is dark with ingested material. This period from August to October is the season when heavy grub feeding may so completely cut off the grass's root system that large pieces of turf can be lifted from the soil like a rug. During October the grubs burrow deep into the soil and rest for the winter. When the soil begins to warm in the spring, they return to the upper layers of soil and feed lightly. After that they enter a short resting stage, then pass through a pupal stage, and after three to four weeks emerge as adult beetles. The treatment for any one species of these grubs will usually be effective against the other species.

  To be most effective, appropriate insecticides should be applied in late summer or very early fall when the grubs are tiny and easily killed. When 8 to 10 grubs are found per square foot, the threshold for chemical treatment has been reached. To examine the turf, cut three sides of a 1-foot square of sod with a spade and roll it back using the uncut side as a hinge. Search through the soil at a depth of 1 inch for tiny grubs ¼ to ½-inch long, not much thicker than lead in a pencil, but with the characteristic shape and color of the older and larger grubs. Insecticides

Figure 11-2. Two of several species of beetles (top) that lay eggs in turf
             and produce grubs (bottom) that feed voraciously on grass
             roots. (Top—*U.S. Dept. of Agriculture Bulletin 53;*
             Bottom—Wisconsin Agricultural Experiment Station)

useful in killing grubs include *Diazinon, Sevin, Oftanol, Turcam, Mocap,*
and *Triumph.* Such insecticides may be purchased in various formulations
for application as sprays or granules. The insecticide selected should be
applied at the dosages and in the manner recommended on the label. It
is well to remember that the grubs are in the soil and the insecticide
must be washed down to a depth of about an inch to do any killing.

 Milky disease spores provide the turf manager with a natural technique
of controlling grubs without the use of insecticides. This milky disease

of grubs is caused by a bacterium (*Bacillus lentimorbus*) and several closely related organisms. This treatment should be made in midsummer, but may be applied any time in late summer or early fall. The spores carried in the dust will infect the grubs as they grow and largely prevent them from feeding on grass roots and emerging as beetles the following summer. Complete control will usually take up to two years, but it is permanent once the milky spores are introduced. This disease is completely harmless to pets, humans, and other warm-blooded animals. The dust containing milky disease spore can be obtained from garden supply stores. This permanent treatment is compatible with the insecticides that kill mature beetles. The infected grubs (larvae of beetles) take on a whitish or milky appearance before death. Spores released upon the death of the grubs persist in the soil for many years and infect new crops of grubs as they feed on grass roots. Conditions of soil, moisture and temperature that are favorable for growth of turfgrasses, also favor propagation and spread of the milky disease of grubs.

- **Billbugs**—This is another group of insects that damage turf by extensive feeding on grass roots. The adults are small beetles ¼ to ¾ of an inch long. They are easily recognized by their long snouts or bills tipped with a pair of strong jaws which they use to feed. Various kinds of

Figure 11-3. **Billbugs and their grubs may increase to such numbers that they seriously damage turf. The adult burrows in grass stems and the grub feeds on grass roots.** (*U.S. Dept. of Agriculture Bulletin 53*)

billbugs range in color from clay yellow to reddish brown to jet black. Beetles burrow into grass stems near the soil surface and also feed on leaves. If abundant enough to cause serious damage, the adults may be found by a close examination of turf at or near ground level where grass appears unhealthy or dying. Under some conditions, the population of billbugs may build up to tremendous numbers and cause rapid and extensive damage to the grass. Prompt treatment should be made of the entire lawn as soon as the infestation is found, since the presence of grubs produced from eggs laid by the billbug adults are certain to cause severe damage. The grubs that feed on grass roots during the summer period can promptly kill the grass. Apply insecticides in late spring or early summer. *Baygon, Diazinon, Dursban,* and *Oftanol* are labeled to control billbugs.

- **Chinch bugs and false chinch bugs**—These are different species of insects

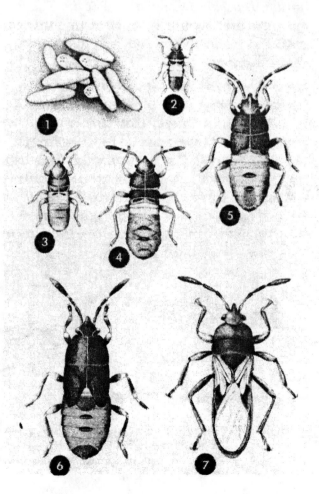

Figure 11-4. Chinchbugs are fairly common pests of turf and damage grass by sucking on plant juice in stems and leaves. Eggs (1), nymphs (2 through 6), do not acquire wings until they reach adulthood (7). (Courtesy, U.S. Dept. of Agriculture)

with similar habits. Both injure grass by sucking juice from plant stems and leaves. However, the true chinch bug is the species that usually damages lawns. Heavily infested lawns first develop yellowish spots which soon become brown dead areas. The adult insect is about $\frac{1}{16}$ of an inch long and mostly black with white wings and markings. They lay eggs that hatch into nymphs which are small-scale replicas of the adult but without wings. The nymphs feed by sucking plant juice from leaves and stems and grow quite rapidly. Nymphs shed their skin four times before they reach the adult stage. Most of the damage to grass is done by the nymphs, and since they are very tiny their depredations may go unnoticed until severe damage has been done. Any unhealthy patches of grass should be examined quite closely, particularly at the margins of the patches where the feeding nymphs are most abundant. If these active little pests are found, treatment should be made promptly.

The following insecticides are effective in controlling chinch bugs: *Turcam, Dursban, Diazinon,* and *Sevin.* These insecticides kill by contact, and therefore, should be applied in sufficient volume and coverage to reach the insect in the sod near the ground surface. Always follow all label directions.

- **Sod webworms**—These pests feed on grass leaves and stems and are capable of severe damage when abundant. The adults are small, whitish or gray moths (millers) that hide in shrubbery during the day and in evening fly over the grass and lay their eggs. The eggs hatch to produce soft-bodied larvae that feed on grass. Sod webworms only feed at night. The worms live in burrows or channels at the soil surface or just below it. They live in the burrows that are reinforced with pieces of grass or silk and only leave to feed on grass crowns, leaves and roots. The first evidence may be the appearance of irregular brown spots. Careful scrutiny will reveal the burrows or channels each inhabited by one or more dirty

Figure 11-5. Sod webworms, armyworms, and cutworms are the larval stages of small moths. The larvae feed on grass stems and leaves and may cause serious damage when abundant. (*U.S. Dept. of Agriculture Bulletin 53*)

white larvae. Some species of webworms burrow into the soil, and come to the surface at night to feed. They may be found by breaking apart some of the sod, and if as many as three or four are found in a 6-inch-square section, an insecticide should be applied promptly to stop damage. Since webworms feed at night, treatments should be applied late in the day.

Insecticides that are effective against sod webworms are: *Diazinon, Propoxur, Turcam, Dursban, Dylox, Oftanol,* and *Sevin.* They may be applied as granules or sprays. Read and follow all label directions!

- **Armyworms and cutworms**—These are the larvae of brown or grayish moths. They customarily fly at night and therefore may go unnoticed. Armyworms are greenish and have black stripes along each side and down the back. When approaching full size, they reach a length of 1 to 2 inches. They feed voraciously, devouring grass down to the ground.

Cutworms are less gregarious but may do a great deal of damage by night feeding. The turf manager should search for these worms whenever bare spots suddenly develop. The various kinds of cutworms are dull-brown, gray, or nearly black, or may be spotted and striped, smooth caterpillars. They are usually found hiding in the upper layer of soil in the daytime. Insecticide applications should be made in late afternoon or early evening when these insects are active. The following insecticides are labeled to control armyworms and cutworms: *Diazinon, Sevin, Dursban,* and *Dylox.*

- **Mole crickets**—These insects are most likely to be serious pests in the South Atlantic and Gulf Coast states from North Carolina to Texas. They are about 1½ inches long, have short, stout forelegs, shovel-like feet, and prominent, beady eyes. They are particularly damaging on new seedings where they feed on grass roots, uprooting the plants and causing rapid drying of soil. One cricket can damage several yards of newly seeded turf in a single night. If a locality has a record of mole cricket damage, it would be well to apply a preventive treatment rather than wait for the damage to appear.

The following insecticides are labeled to control mole crickets: *Diazinon, Propoxur, Turcam, Oftanol* and *Sevin.* Always read and follow all label directions!

- **Leaf hoppers**—These are tiny insects that fly or hop short distance when disturbed. They are less than ¼-inch long and may be colored green, yellow, or brownish gray. They injure grass by sucking sap from the grass stems and leaves, particularly on new seedings, and may cause

Figure 11-6. Mole crickets attack turf in warmer regions. A single cricket may damage several square yards in one night. (*U.S. Dept. of Agriculture Bulletin 53*)

Figure 11-7. Pesticides are very helpful in a turf management program. Always read and follow all label directions. (Courtesy, Terra International, Inc., Professional Products)

extensive damage. Leaf hoppers are most abundant in warm weather and the appearance of damaged seedings may resemble drought injury; however, if there are substantial numbers of the leaf hoppers present, it is safe to assume they are causing the damage.

Insecticide sprays to use on leaf hoppers include *Malathion*, *Sevin*, and *Diazinon*. Always read and follow all label directions!

TURF PESTS THAT PRODUCE UNSIGHTLY CONDITIONS

These categories of pests include earthworms, ants, moles, gophers, and crayfish (on some soils). They are not particularly damaging to the grass and may actually be beneficial in some instances.

- **Earthworms**—These worms burrow through the soil, ingesting soil along with vegetable material and generally improving the permeability of the soil. However, in moist soil, and particularly after a rain, they come to the surface and excrete casts in abundance. Since earthworms feed through the entire soil profile to the depth occupied by grass roots, they are very difficult control. One should decide whether it may not be sufficient to break up the worm casts by pulling a flexible steel mat across the turf area whenever this becomes necessary. The worms serve

Figure 11-8. Ants are merely a nuisance because of the ant hills that mar the turf surface.

as food for many birds and this value, plus the benefits of improving soil structure, may offset the nuisance of the worm casts.

- **Ants**—Except for fire ants and harvester ants that have invaded some states, most ants are merely a nuisance because of the ant hills that mar the turf surface. Individual ant hills may be treated with a drenching of *Diazinon* or *Sevin* to destroy the nests.

  Fire ants (in certain southern states) and harvester ants (in the West) not only damage grass, but they bite people and animals. These qualities constitute them as vicious pests. Special control measures are required to control these specific kinds of ants, and advice should be sought from the county agricultural agent.

Figure 11-9. Moles dig tunnels near the soil surface.

- **Moles**—These animals dig tunnels near the soil surface. Their main food source is earthworms, not grubs as previously thought. The only effective control is traps. Many "home remedies" are reported to work, but under scientific tests only traps have been proven effective.

PESTS THAT INHABIT TURF AND ATTACK PEOPLE

These pests should not be tolerated because of the misery they cause or the health hazards they create for humans. They include bees, wasps and yellow jackets, chiggers, fleas, and ticks. Fortunately, there are effective insecticide treatments for these pests.

- **Wild bees, wasps and yellow jackets**—These are different species of insects that have the common characteristic of attacking people and some pets when disturbed. Their stings are painful and may be quite dangerous for those who are sensitive to the venom injected. Certain of these species prefer grass sod for making nests and there is no suitable alternative to prompt poisoning when a nest is located. Usually a drenching of the nest in the evening, when the insects are quiescent, and sealing of the entrance with dirt produces a good kill. The exterminator should wear protective clothing in the event that some insects escape and attack while treatment is underway.

    The insecticides found effective for these pests include *Sevin* and *Diazinon.*

- **Chiggers (red bugs)**—These are tiny and seldom seen, but they are found in grassy areas throughout the southern states and as far north as Iowa, Illinois, and Pennsylvania by midsummer. They crawl unseen onto people whenever they touch the ground, attach themselves to the skin, and release a poison that causes intense itching and irritation. Their presence in lawns virtually denies the use of these pleasant areas to people throughout the summer.

    Chiggers are quite effectively controlled by appropriate insecticides such as *Diazinon* and *Sevin*, applied as dusts or sprays. It is well to make an adequate application before the "chigger season" begins and to repeat this each year. If well treated in spring, it is unlikely that a second treatment will be needed in the same summer.

- **Ticks**—These pests may inhabit turf, especially if the turf adjoins woods or open fields. The ticks arrive on the bodies of wild animals, rodents, and pets, and survive for extended periods awaiting an opportunity to attach themselves to another host. Unless recently fed, these ticks, of which there are many kinds, are quite small and easily go unnoticed because of their camouflage coloring. Nearly all of them attack man when given an opportunity. Not only are ticks a revolting type of parasite, but their bites are painful and they may transmit serious diseases such as tick-fever and tularemia.

    Turf areas may be freed of ticks and kept free by application of appropriate insecticides. A spring application may be followed by a second treatment in July or August to kill those ticks present and any that are brought in and dropped by any type of carrier. Effective insecticides are the same as those used against chiggers; *Sevin* and *Diazinon*.

PRECAUTIONS TO TAKE IN THE USE OF INSECTICIDES

All insecticides are poisons and must be carefully used to preclude injury to people, domestic animals, and desirable kinds of wildlife. When properly used, they are safe and effective.

Insecticides used improperly may be harmful to humans and animals.

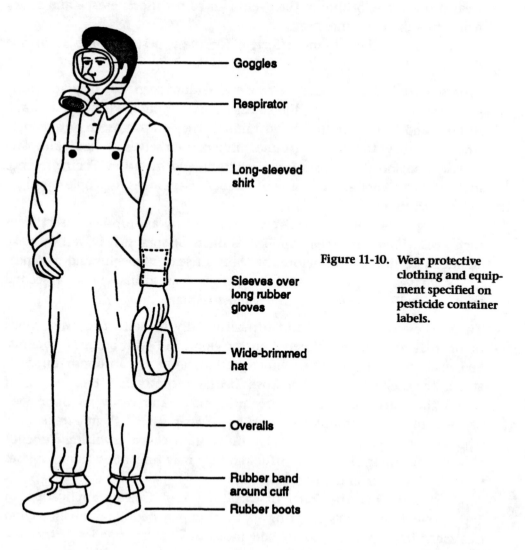

Goggles

Respirator

Long-sleeved shirt

Sleeves over long rubber gloves

Wide-brimmed hat

Overalls

Rubber band around cuff

Rubber boots

Figure 11-10. Wear protective clothing and equipment specified on pesticide container labels.

1. Use them only when needed and handle them with care. Follow the directions and heed all precautions on the labels.

2. Keep insecticides in closed, well-labeled containers in a dry place. Store them where they will not contaminate food or feed, and where children and animals cannot reach them.

3. When handling an insecticide, wear rubber gloves.

4. Avoid repeated or prolonged contact of insecticide with skin.

5. Wear the protective clothing and equipment specified on the container label. Avoid prolonged inhalation of insecticide dusts or mists.

6. Avoid spilling insecticide concentrate on skin, and keep it out of the eyes, nose, and mouth. If spilled on skin, wash it off immediately with soap and water. If spilled on clothing, remove the clothing immediately and wash the skin thoroughly. Launder the clothing before wearing it again.

7. Don't let insecticides drift to an area where they might injure people or animals, or contaminate food or water.

8. After an insecticide has been applied, do not allow children and pets on the grass until the insecticide has been washed off by sprinkling, and the grass has dried completely.

9. After handling an insecticide, do not eat, drink, or smoke until hands and face are washed. Wash any exposed skin immediately after applying an insecticide.

10. Dispose of empty insecticide containers according to label directions.

EXPLANATION OF TECHNICAL TERMS

- **Adult** describes the stage when most insects are capable of reproduction. Examples of the adult stages of different insects are beetles, moths, and butterflies.

- **Larval stage** is the stage when most insect feeding and growth occur. Depending on the kind of insect, this may be a grub or worm. For example, armyworms, cutworms, sod webworms, and white grubs are the larval stages of serious turf pests.

- **Nymph stage** is an intermediate stage in the life of insects that have an incomplete metamorphosis life cycle. Thus, in chinch bugs, the growth stage is a nymph that resembles an adult but is smaller. Nymphs pass through several molts before becoming fully grown adults.

- **Pupal stage** is the resting stage typical of many types of insects which occurs after larval growth has been completed and during which there is a metamorphosis or transformation. Upon emergence from the pupal stage, the insect is a fully developed adult capable of reproduction.

- **Insecticides** are those pesticides used to control certain insects. This is particularly true since many insects are beneficial and should be protected. Of all the types of pesticides, it is the insecticides that offer the greatest hazard to the health of people. Because of the health hazards, insecticides are carefully regulated by both state and federal laws as to permissible use. Always read and follow all label directions.

Chapter 12

CONTROLLING DISEASES ON TURFGRASSES

The turf manager, whether responsible for home lawns, parks, athletic fields, or industrial lawns, has already taken the major steps in disease control when adopting a sound system of turf management. Although there are many turfgrass diseases, only a few are likely to cause serious problems on lawns.

SELECTION OF GRASSES

The selection of grasses suited to the climatic regions and the particular turf areas has been discussed in earlier chapters. The principles of soil management and the proper use of fertilizers have also been outlined. Both help to develop resistance to diseases and increase the ability of grass to recover rapidly from outbreaks that may occur as the result of weather conditions that favor a particular disease organism. The use of grass mixtures is an asset, since different species will have different degrees of susceptibility to a specific pathogen. The disease is held in check by the interspersing of resistant plants between susceptible plants. Within a species, such as Kentucky bluegrass, the practice of planting a mixture of cultivars is an asset in avoiding the spread of disease. One or more of the cultivars in a mixture of these may be expected to survive a severe disease attack.

AVOID CLOSE CUTTING

Most of the turf diseases attack the grass leaves. Turf that is cut too short is less able to endure attacks of leaf disease and make a strong recovery. Closely cut turf, such as bentgrass putting greens must receive fungicide treatments to protect the turfgrass from diseases. Grass cut at $2^1/_2$ to 3 inches long can develop the strength needed to resist disease damage.

REMOVE CLIPPINGS

Grass clippings should be removed promptly after mowing whenever they are heavy enough to produce a mat for more than a day. Clippings that dry out promptly and sift down to the soil are not a problem. A mat of clippings will maintain the humidity and provide a nutrient supply sufficient to culture a heavy growth of disease fungi that promptly attack the living grass beneath the mat.

Figure 12-1. Prompt removal of grass clippings is a good disease prevention practice, particularly in wet weather or in areas of heavy grass growth. (Courtesy, John Tonsor)

AVOID EXCESS MOISTURE

Excess moisture is an invitation to disease organisms, particularly in warm weather. Waterlogged soils should be artificially drained if they are incapable of adequate internal drainage. Turf should be watered early enough in the day to allow grass leaves to dry completely before nightfall; wet leaves at night in the summer can foster disease development. When watering lawns, the soil should be well moistened to a depth of six or more inches, but no more should be added until these soil reserves are nearly exhausted. Frequent light watering, particularly in the evening in warm weather, may stimulate disease on turfgrass.

IMPROVE AIR CIRCULATION

Many turf areas are partially enclosed by trees, shrubs, or other plantings which can be a hindrance to air movements. Such poorly ventilated areas not only stay moist for a long time each day, but they also tend to be excessively warm in the afternoon and evening. These conditions are unfavorable for good grass growth, but are quite favorable for the development of grass diseases. The remedy is to permit freer air movement by pruning and removal of some planting to open channels of circulation. Watering should be limited to that actually needed by the plants.

MOWING IN COOL SEASONS

Mowing practices may either foster disease injury or protect against outbreaks. Mowing should be done regularly before the grass gets so tall that cutting will remove more than half the total leaf area. Tall, neglected turf that is suddenly cut short has literally been scalped. Practically all new leaf growth must be made at the risk of exhausting food reserves in stems and crowns, often in a period when soil moisture is deficient. The grass may require weeks to recover from such scalping and from the diseases that attack the new tender growth.

Since some serious grass diseases attack turf in the cool weather of late fall, winter, and spring, the mowing schedule should be continued in fall since significant growth is made during this time. Do not permit a heavy mat of leaves to accumulate as winter approaches, since such mats favor "snow mold" and similar diseases. Turfgrasses do not need the mulching effect of uncut tops to protect against winter weather.

The appropriate way to develop strength is to fertilize adequately at the appropriate seasons. The management practices recommended in earlier chapters will often reduce the occurrence and severity of grass diseases. It is unlikely that damage from turf disease will become sufficiently serious, on a specific lawn area, to warrant special treatment. However, there is a necessity to make a diagnosis of a serious disease when it appears, so that appropriate treatment can be applied. Also, it is necessary to distinguish between insect damage and disease injury. A careful examination of the turfgrass and the soil just below the surface should reveal the presence of any important insect pests. In other words, there should be reasonable evidence of disease injury before undertaking treatment for control of the disease.

Figure 12-2. Test plots for disease treatments. (Courtesy, Terra International, Inc., Professional Products)

IMPORTANT DISEASES AND TREATMENTS[1]

The turf manager should be on the lookout for the following grass diseases:

- **Leaf spot**, formerly called **helminthosporium**, is caused by a type of fungus that attacks the lower (older) leaves of grass and the basal leaf sheaths and stems. This disease is now called **Drechslera Disease**. The disease first appears as dark reddish or purplish spots on leaves and stems at the points where the fungus invades. When severely attacked, the leaves, stems, and crowns will discolor and die. There are many kinds of these fungi. The different species and varieties of turfgrasses have differing degrees of resistance to the pathogens. It is useful to plant mixtures of grasses for preventing or retarding the spread of this disease. Frequently, the turf manager does not notice the damage to the grass until it is seriously thinned out and weakened. By then, the epidemic may have subsided and the injury might easily be charged to drought or to weed encroachment (since weeds suddenly flourish when grass no longer offers competition).

    This disease is most likely to occur during the cool, moist weather of spring and fall, but it may be found in summer when cooler

---

[1]For color photographs of diseases, see the color photo section in this book.

Turfgrass Disease Color Plates

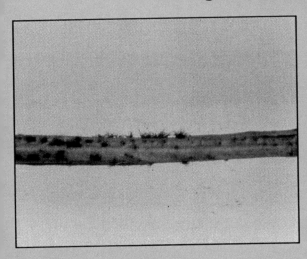

Anthracnose

Pink Snow Mold

Necrotic Ring Spot

Slime Mold

Rust

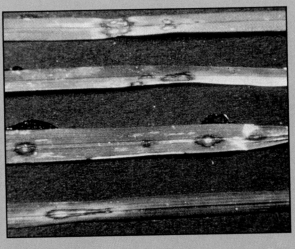

Melting Out

I

Turfgrass Disease Color Plates

Leaf Spot

Leaf Spot

Leaf Spot

Powdery Mildew

Powdery Mildew

Powdery Mildew

Turfgrass Disease Color Plates

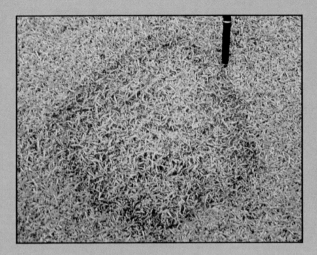

Red Thread

Red Thread

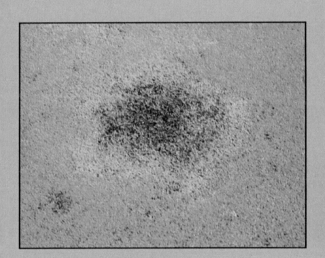

Brown Patch

Brown Patch

Fairy Ring

Fairy Ring

III

Turfgrass Disease Color Plates

Dollar Spot

Dollar Spot

Pythium Blight

Pythium Blight

Pythium Blight

Pythium Blight

IV

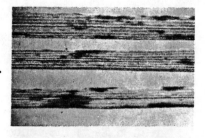

Figure 12-3. Leaf spot disease on tall fescue grass leaves.

Figure 12-4. Leaf spot disease on bluegrass.

Figure 12-5. Extensive damage by leaf spot disease. Leaves in the light-colored areas are largely dead.

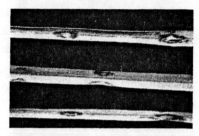

Figure 12-6. Leaf spot disease in early spring. (Courtesy, Wilmington Delaware Country Club)

temperatures and moisture are favorable. To minimize damage, it is important to practice mowing at longer lengths and to provide enough fertilizer for sustained growth without over stimulation. Healthy, vigorous grass will usually recover from such disease attacks, but excessive nitrogen fertilizer stimulation makes the grass more susceptible. All clippings should be removed where this disease is prevalent, since the fungus is favored by presence of moisture and by mats of fresh green clippings. Chemical control is accomplished by using one of the following fungicides: *Acti-dione, Daconil 2787, Chipco 26019, Touché,* and *Dyrene.* Read and follow all label instructions and precautions.

- **Summer patch, Fusarium patch**, and **Fusarium syndrome** are all names used to describe this elusive turf disease. This has been called **Fusarium roseum** or **Fusarium tricinctum** for many years; however, most turf experts are now calling it summer patch (*Phialophora graminicola*). The term frog-eye will best describes the appearance of turf infected with summer patch. Dead circles, 12 inches in diameter, with small tufts of green grass in the center best describe the look of this disease. Summer patch can attack most cool season turf species but Kentucky bluegrass is very susceptible to this disease. However, many of the new Kentucky bluegrass cultivars are resistant to this disease. Summer patch is a hot weather disease usually seen when the day temperatures are above 85 degrees. Cultural controls may reduce the severity of this disease. A light application of fertilizer, $1/2$ pound nitrogen per 1000 square feet, each month during the summer can help reduce the severity of summer patch. Maintaining good soil moisture by irrigation and aerifying the soil to improve root growth may also reduce the severity of this disease. Chemical control is very difficult after this disease starts attacking turfgrass. Some turf managers are having success with preventative applications of fungicides, making one application in April and the second in May. The fungicides most useful in treating this disease are *Rubigan, Chipco 26019, Fungo 50,* and *Cleary 3336.* Always read and follow all label directions.

- **Brownpatch** is a disease caused by the fungus *Rhizoctonia*, which attacks many grasses and is most prevalent in warm humid weather. The sus-

Figure 12-7. **Large brownpatch on bentgrass. The turf is discolored but not dead and will recover if treated promptly with fungicide.**

Figure 12-8. **Large brownpatch showing how diseased spots grow together to form large irregular blotches. Prompt treatment will save the grass.**

ceptible period for brownpatch is much longer in southern than in northern regions. It is most damaging when lush growth has been produced by excessive use of soluble nitrogen fertilizers and by frequent watering. The disease affects irregular patches of varying sizes, turning the grass brown. With light attacks, the fungus kills the leaves but not the stems, and the turf may make a recovery in two to three weeks when cooler, dry weather returns. However, if the weather is warm and humid the fungus will attack the stems and crowns and kill the grass. Unlike some other turf diseases, the dead grass remains erect and does not lie flat. In case of doubt as to diagnosis, examine the turf in early morning while the dew is on to note filmy, whitish fungus threads at the edges of spreading patches; if present, the disease is brownpatch. The predisposing factors are excessive stimulation by nitrogen fertilizer in warm seasons, unwise watering that keeps soil and grass continuously moist (particularly at night) and failure to remove clippings promptly.

The same fungicides are used to control this disease that are used to control leaf spot, root-rot, and fading-out disease. Use one of the following, at the dosages recommended by the manufacturer: *Dyrene, Fore, Daconil 2787, Rubigan, Chipco 26019,* or *PCNB*. In prolonged periods of warm, humid weather, it may be necessary to repeat treatments of highly susceptible grass every 10 to 14 days.

- **Grease spot** and **cottony blight** diseases are caused by species of the *Pythium* fungus, and the term "pythium disease" has become widely used. These diseases occur in humid areas, and are destructive when temperatures stay above 70F at night. Pythium is most serious on newly established seedlings, but may attack grass of any age. The first signs of the disease are the appearance in the morning of circular spots, sometimes merging, that has a blackened appearance at first but fade to a light brown during the day. Not only are the leaves killed, but stems and crowns die within 24 hours. Leaves and stems become water-soaked, mat together, and appear slimy which gives a general appearance of grease spots, although the cause is the invading fungus.

This disease is so disastrous on young grass seedlings that new plantings should be avoided in "pythium weather," and undertaken in cooler periods of early spring or in fall. On established turf, all practices should minimize wet soil and foliage that stimulate the pythium organisms. The fungicides found most useful against pythium disease are *Subdue, Aliette, Banol, and Koban*. Prolonged periods of weather favoring this disease may make it necessary to repeat treatments every 7 to 10 days. Always read and follow all label information.

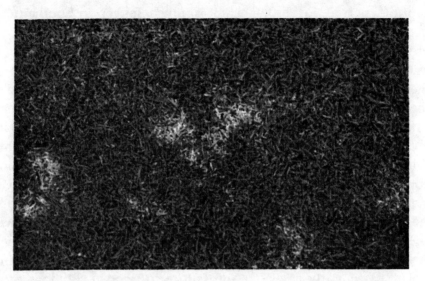

Figure 12-9.   Dollar spot disease on creeping bentgrass in June.

- **Dollar spot** is a disease caused by *Sclerotinia* fungus that is particularly serious on bentgrass turf on putting greens, but may occur in other turf. It produces bleached spots about the size of a silver dollar, which accounts for the name. At the start of infection, the invaded spots are dark and water-soaked but they soon turn brown and later bleach almost white. If the disease is noted in the early stages of attack, treatment with appropriate fungicides may halt invasion and permit prompt recovery. After the grass has died in the invaded spots, healing will require grass growth from surrounding areas. Early treatment with appropriate fungicides is desirable, and treatment will protect the grass against further spread of the fungus. Nitrogen fertilizer applications will help to prevent this disease.

    The fungicides useful against this disease are: *Acti-dione, Daconil 2787, Touché, Rubigan,* and *Chipco 26019.* Apply at dosages and in the manner prescribed on the label.

- **Rust,** caused by the fungus *Puccinia graminis,* and **powdery mildew,** caused by the fungus *Erysiphe graminis,* are sometimes found on Kentucky bluegrass. The disease attacks are spectacular but usually short-lived, and rarely kill the grass. Rust produces a coating of reddish-colored pustules that nearly cover the grass leaves and make an unsightly appearance. Powdery mildew makes a whitish-gray coating on the leaves, and may kill the invaded leaves. Warm humid weather is favorable for development of these diseases, and any practices that accentuate high humidity and wet grass leaves are undesirable.

Both rust and powdery mildew are controlled by *Acti-dione Thiram.* However, the application of fungicides is seldom required to control these diseases.

- **Snow mold** shows up in late fall or early spring as matted patches of dead grass 1 to 12 inches across. The disease is caused by the fungus *Fusarium nivale* that is unique because it develops only in moist grass at temperatures below 40°F. It often occurs under snow blankets when the soil is not frozen, but also develops without a snow cover. A similar blight is caused by the fungus *Typhula itoana*.

  If past experience has shown the prevalence of this disease, a preventive fungicide should be applied before the onset of cold weather. The fungicides used for this purpose are: *Cleary 3336, PCNB, Chipco 26019, Daconil 2787,* and *Tersan SP.*

- **Slime molds** create a spectacular appearance by coating the leaves with dusty, bluish-gray, black, or yellowish masses. These fungi feed largely on dead organic matter and climb the live grass leaves to produce fruiting bodies and spores. Slime molds usually occur during wet weather or when turf watering is overdone. The molds may be dissipated by a strong stream of water and fungicides are not recommended.

Figure 12-10. **Typhula Snow Mold (Gray or Speckled) structures are sclerotia, resting structures, of the fungal pathogen *Typhula incarnata*.**

POOR TURF WHEN NOT CAUSED BY FUNGI

Before undertaking to control a suspected disease of turf, it is appropriate to find out the actual cause of the unfavorable condition. There are many turf conditions that can be mistaken as turf diseases. The following are examples of other turfgrass injury: fertilizer burn, female dog urine injury, insect injury, injury from misapplication of pesticides, scalping with a mower, and thatch accumulation. These problems have been covered in earlier chapters. Since diseases are caused by fungi that require specific conditions of weather and grass and produce unique symptoms in the turf, these should be the guides to reason.

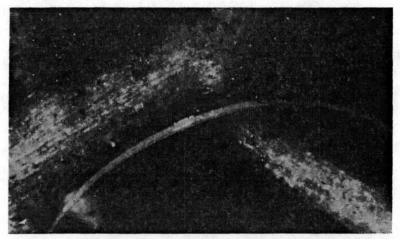

Figure 12-11.   The thread-like worm shown above is a nematode, greatly enlarged with a microscope. They invade the roots and crowns of grass and greatly reduce the grass vigor. (Courtesy, U.S. Dept. of Agriculture)

Nematode damage is more common in warmer regions, but occurs in other regions also. This problem is caused by microscopic worms that invade the roots and crowns of grass and greatly reduce the grass vigor. Fortunately, many improved varieties of bermudagrass and the zoysias are resistant to nematodes. A careful examination of roots of infested plants will usually reveal small nodules or swelling on the roots and also a poorly developed root system that seriously weakens the turf.

Treatments for nematodes should be made when soil temperatures at depths of 1 to 2 inches are above 65°F. The chemical effective against nematodes is *Nemacur*. It should be applied as directed on the label.

EXPLANATION OF TECHNICAL TERMS

Common names of diseases—Diseases are usually caused by a specific pathogen—a particular species of a fungus, bacterium, actinomyces or virus. Diseases have typical appearances, as illustrated by brownpatch, snow mold, etc. Since the visible symptoms are sometimes similar, although the pathogen is different, it often becomes necessary to identify the disease by the causal agent. Thus we speak of Drechslera leaf spot—which means it is a leaf disease caused by the fungus named *Drechslera*. Although such language is complex, it is useful in treating diseases to be certain of the causal agent.

- **Nematodes** are tiny slender worms, so small they can only be seen with a microscope. Some of the more vigorous strains of bermudagrass are resistant to soil-inhabiting nematodes.

- **Thatch** is the term used to describe the accumulation of dead roots and stems, mostly at the soil surface or immediately above.

Chapter 13

TURF IRRIGATION

The irrigation of crops dates back more than 5,000 years. Plants combine carbon dioxide with water in the photosynthetic process to make a sugar compound needed by plants for growth and development. Water helps to cool plant tissue by a process called transpiration. Plants also use water for the absorption of nutrients and the movement of these nutrients within the plant.

For years people have relied on nature, through rainfall, to supply the necessary water for good turfgrass growth. Only in the past 50 to 60 years has this natural rainfall been supplemented by the artificial application of water by sprinkler irrigation systems. The first fully automatic golf course irrigation systems were installed in California in the early 1950s. Many years after golf course irrigation systems became common place installing automatic home-lawn systems started.

SOIL WATER RELATIONSHIP

Rainfall will normally supply the grass plant with needed water; but

Figure 13-1. Irrigating turfgrass at a California sod farm.

159

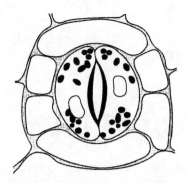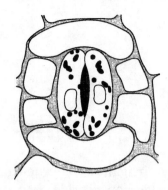

Figure 13-2. Stomata with turgid guard cell and pore open (left) and flaccid guard cell with pore closed (right). Stomata regulate transpiration and gas exchange. An open stomata allows water to pass into the air, increasing the need of the plant for water.

when rainfall does not provide enough water then an irrigation system must be installed. Turf irrigation systems replace soil moisture lost by transpiration of turf leaves and evaporation of water from the soil surface. The term evaportranspiration (ET) combines the loss of water from the soil surface by evaporation with the diffusion of water through stomata in the leaves of plants by transpiration into one easy number to use.

When the ET rate exceeds the rainfall (RF) then the turf should be irrigated. ET rates on hot, dry July days can exceed 7½ inches per month. For example, if an average of 3 inches of rain can be expected during the month of July, then 7½" ET – 3" RF = 4½" of irrigation required on this turf during the month of July. The 4½ inches of irrigation should be spread out evenly through the entire month. Areas not receiving any rainfall will require applying the entire 7½ inches of water using an irrigation system.

Soil type and soil texture both affect the watering holding capacity and water movement in the soil. Sandy soils allow water to quickly move from the surface into the soil. However, sandy soils cannot retain a good reservoir of moisture for good turfgrass growth. Apply heavy rates of irrigation frequently, every two or three days, to keep turfgrass looking good when growing on sandy soils.

Water moves slowly into clay soils because the many small pore spaces are hard to wet, but once wet, clay soils retain large quantities of water. Apply water slowly to clay soils. The maximum run time for sprinklers will be approximately 10 minutes. Repeat this cycle every 30 minutes until the required water is applied. Soil type will affect not only the total water required by turf but also the rate that this water is applied to the soil.

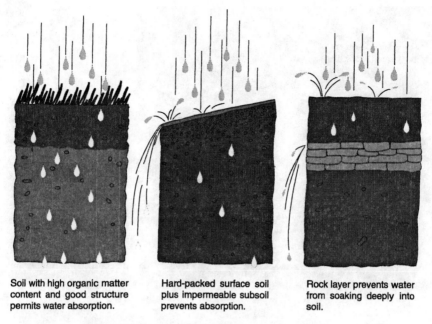

| Soil with high organic matter content and good structure permits water absorption. | Hard-packed surface soil plus impermeable subsoil prevents absorption. | Rock layer prevents water from soaking deeply into soil. |

Figure 13-3. Water infiltration and percolation.

When to Water Turf

Try to water turf between 10:00 p.m. and 6:00 a.m. for the following reasons. The ET rate is much lower at night because it is cooler and usually there is less wind. Lower water use at night by all city water customers results in higher pressure for sprinkler systems and therefore better coverage. Night watering reduces the incidence of turf disease problems. Watering at night using hoses and movable sprinklers is not possible for most home-owners. Today, automatic irrigation systems can be programmed to turn on and off at any time of the day or night.

Irrigate turf when 60 to 80 percent of the available water has been used by the plants or when wilt is first seen on plants. Turfgrass leaves turn bluish under mild water stress. If not watered, the blue color will change to yellow, moderate stress, and finally to brown. Always water turf when leaves turn blue, but before they turn yellow, for best turf growth.

RESIDENTIAL IRRIGATION SYSTEMS

Spray-head sprinklers generally emit single or double fans of water in a fixed pattern. These patterns usually only cover part of a circle and are called part-circle. Some spray-heads have a fixed pattern while other have

Figure 13-4. Pop-up turf
irrigation head.
(Courtesy, Rain
Bird)

a variable or adjustable arc. Stream sprays, another type of sprinkler,
distribute water in numerous individual fingers or streams and usually have
fixed arcs of coverage. A third sprinkler called pop-up rotary heads is fast
becoming the choice for home irrigation systems.

Pop-up rotating sprinklers have a single pair of nozzles, which revolve
to distribute water over the area of coverage. Both part-circle and full-circle
units are available. Pop-up sprinklers come in a wide range of operating
pressure from 25 to 100 psi range and with water coverage 10 to more
than 100 feet of radius. Rotary sprinkler heads usually apply water more
slowly than spray heads because the water is spread out over greater areas.
Irrigation systems using rotating pop-up sprinklers require fewer heads than
systems using spray-head sprinklers.

Electric operated water valves called solenoid valves and automatic
controllers make up the modern turf irrigation system. An electric impulse
delivered through a control wire opens and closes these remote solenoid
valves that allow water to flow to the sprinkler head.

Most states require the installation of a backflow prevention device on
all home irrigation systems to prevent contamination of drinking water
(potable water) with pesticides and other chemicals used on the turf.
Contaminated water can be forced to "backflow" through irrigation pipes
into a potable water system and endanger the public health. A licensed
plumber can correctly install these devises. A yearly check will ensure the
continued safe operation of all backflow prevention devices.

Galvanized steel pipe installed exclusively in the past has been replaced

Figure 13-5. A backflow valve prevents contamination of city water during irrigation.

by newer plastic pipe materials. Polyethylene (PE) pipe is a tough, black, waxy material derived by combining hydrogen and carbon. PE pipe is flexible and is sold in 100 and 400 foot coils. Its chief advantages are, excellent impact strength, flexibility, and resistance from damage by freezing. Install plastic insert fittings in PE pipe using stainless steel "radiator" type hose clamps.

Polyvinyl Chloride (PVC) is made by combining coke, lime and salt. It is the toughest and most durable plastic pipe available. PVC pipe is sold in straight pieces 20- or 40-foot long. Solvent welding or glue joints hold the socket-type pipe fittings to the pipe.

Cover all plastic pipe used for home irrigation systems with a minimum of 8 inches of soil. Remove dirt from pipe ends and from fittings before coating both with a "cleaning solution." After cleaning, apply the "glue" or solvent cement to the fitting socket then the pipe end. Push the fitting onto the pipe and twist one quarter of a turn to evenly distribute the solvent and hold joint for 30 to 60 seconds. Do not use an excessive amount of solvent as this only serves to weaken the pipe. Wait 24 hours after completing all joints before testing with full water pressure.

Residential Irrigation Controllers

All controllers have several similar features: a day-of-the-week clock to regulate on which day water is applied, a twenty-four-hour electric clock to regulate the time of day sprinklers operate, and a station clock to control

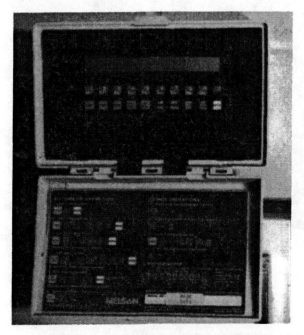

Figure 13-6. Home lawn irrigation controller.

Figure 13-7. Electric shock protection from a GFI Device.

the time each valve is turned on. Electromechanical and solid-state are the two major kinds of controllers used today.

Electromechanical controllers use electric clocks to mechanically turn switches on and off to control solenoid valves. The sound of switches clicking on and off can be heard as these units run. Solid-state controllers use modern electronic circuits to turn on solenoid valves without mechanical switches.

The term "station" describes a single electric switch in a controller that turns on a solenoid valve. Each station is similar to separate light switches in a home, one that turns on a bedroom light and a different switch that turns on the kitchen light. Small controllers used in residential lawn irrigation systems have four or six separate stations that each turn on a separate solenoid valve. Install the controller so the sprinklers operated by the unit are visible. This greatly simplifies system operation tests during installation and later during normal maintenance. However, most residential sprinkler controllers are located out of sight in the garage area. Most city ordinances require the installation of a ground fault interrupter (GFI) on the 117 volt AC receptacle used by the irrigation controller. This additional safety device will prevent accidental electrical shocks from the irrigation system.

Between the controller and the electric solenoid valve that feed the sprinklers, a network of valve control wires exist. Connect each valve to the controller with two wires, its own individual power or control wire and the "common" or "ground" wire. The common wire is connected to and shared by all the valves and completes the circuit back to the controller.

These wires conduct low voltage current, usually 24 volts AC to energize the solenoid on the valve. A solenoid is simply a coil of copper wire that, when energized, lifts a plunger to open a control port in the valve. When the control port opens it allows water pressure above the diaphragm in the valve's upper portion, or bonnet, to bleed off down stream. Most residential systems use a number 16 gauge control wire. Install larger size wire on large estate or light-commercial irrigation systems.

GOLF COURSE IRRIGATION SYSTEMS

Golf course irrigation systems are complex and costly capital investments. Properly designed, installed, and operated irrigation systems provide golfers the quality turf that they want. Automatic irrigation systems consist of fixed pop-up sprinkler heads automatically activated by solenoid water valves turned on by a control devise.

Golf course irrigation systems operate on a low-voltage 24 volts. Most city ordinances require the installation of a ground fault interrupter (GFI) on the 117 volt AC receptacle used by the irrigation controller. The automatic irrigation system may be integrated with an automatic sensing unit that monitors soil moisture levels to decide watering requirements.

The golf course superintendent establishes the specific day, time of day, and operating duration for each solenoid valve that feeds water to one or more sprinklers. Automatic irrigation systems apply water more accurately than manual valve systems. When a green requires 10 minutes of irrigation, the controller applies 10 minutes not 15 minutes of water to the green. This can save large quantities of water during the year.

Modern irrigation systems use remote control valves connected to one or more sprinkler heads. These valves are electrically controlled by the satellite control unit. The manner in which the automatic valve is actuated is termed either normally open or normally closed. Should an electric control line be broken in a normally closed system, the valve will remain closed and no water will flood the green. Flooding of turf can occur when normally open valve systems control lines are broken.

Valve-in-head sprinkler design installs a solenoid valve in each sprinkler head. The electric valve is incorporated in the base of the sprinkler head housing. This design allows individual control of sprinkler heads. Today most golf course irrigation systems use valve-in-head sprinklers.

Golf Course Irrigation Controllers

Controllers have developed from simple clocks sending a signal to one valve to sophisticated computer driven units that can control hundreds of valves at once.

Electromechanical controllers use electric clocks to mechanically turn switches on and off to control solenoid valves. The sound of switches clicking on and off can be heard as these units run. Solid-state controllers use modern electronic circuits to turn on solenoid valves without mechanical switches.

The individual irrigation control units, called satellites, are similar in design to the residential controllers, but usually have 12 or more control stations. Satellites provide irrigation control for the sprinklers on one or two greens, tees, and fairways. All sprinklers controlled by the satellite should be visible from the controller location. Satellite controllers operate independently or may be controlled by a master controller unit.

The master controller turns on each satellite providing a single location for controlling all sprinklers on the golf course. Both electromechanical and solid-state satellite controllers are commonly installed today. Golf course irrigation controllers have: day-of-the-week clocks to regulate which day(s)

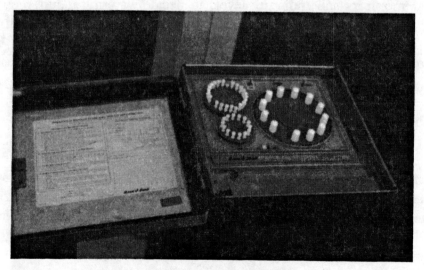

**Figure 13-8. Solid-state satellite golf course irrigation controller.
(Courtesy, Danville Country Club)**

Figure 13-9. A computer irrigation controller for a golf course.

water is applied, twenty-four-hour electric clocks to regulate the time of day sprinklers operate, and station clocks to control the time each valve is turned on.

In the past most satellites were hard wired to the master controller, that is, control cables ran underground from the controller to each satellite. Today, complete radio-controlled satellite systems, no hard wiring, are installed. A soft ware program installed on a personal computer in the superintendent's office is really the master irrigation controller.

Computer control systems provide many additional features not available with simple electromechanical controllers. Optional sensors add an extra level of control to the irrigation system. Rain sensors, tensiometers to measure soil moisture, wind speed meters, and other sensors can be programmed into the system. The irrigation controller can register the precise quantity of any rainfall and shut off sprinklers in those areas where it is raining. If it only rains for a brief period, the controller will resume the irrigation schedule after the rain.

INSTALLING IRRIGATION CONTROL LINES

Electric cable comes in a variety of gauge sizes, including 10- and 12-gauge types. The smaller the cable gauge size number the larger the cable, thus the more electricity it will carry. The long distance between controller and valve requires installing number 10-gauge wire on golf course

Figure 13-10. Installing control wire on golf course.

irrigation systems. Follow all manufactures recommendations on cable selection.

Install control lines in the pipe trenches to one side of the pipe when possible. Placing electric control lines on top of the irrigation pipe increase the chance of damage when digging up the pipe to make plumbing repairs. Golf course irrigation systems are complex and costly capital investments. Properly designed, installed, and operated irrigation systems provide quality turf. Automatic irrigation systems consist of fixed, pop-up sprinkler heads automatically activated by solenoid water valves turned on by a control devise.

Always install cable according to the engineer and manufacturer's specification and carefully check all connections before backfilling the trench. Splice all wire using special connectors that provide a watertight connection. This practice will eliminate future electrical problems from bad electrical connections.

Chapter 14

SPECIAL TURF PROBLEMS AND RENOVATING POOR TURF

TURF FOR PARTIALLY SHADED AREAS

Nearly all home lawns and many parks have some areas where grass is grown with difficulty because of limited exposure to direct sunlight. Even the most tolerant grasses require some direct sunlight daily for healthy growth and survival. Unless there are at least two hours of direct sunlight on partially shaded areas between 8:00 a.m. and 6:00 p.m., it is unlikely that turfgrasses will produce satisfactory cover. For continuously shaded areas some other type of plant cover, such as ivy, myrtle, pachysandra, or other shade plants, should be considered.

Tree Shading

Some trees such as ash, linden, honey locust, and oak allow a good deal of sunlight to filter through the crown to meet the minimum needs of shade-tolerant grasses. Other species such as the Norway maple make a dense canopy that completely shades the ground. Where the shade is dense, some improvement can be achieved by pruning the trees each year to heights of 6 to 10 feet above the ground and thinning out the crown. Pruning is not an adequate corrective measure if the area is over-planted with trees. If there is desire to have both trees and grass, eventually it becomes necessary to remove enough trees to meet the light needs of shade-tolerant grasses. No other treatments will take the place of adequate sunlight. Clearly, the correction of light deficiency is more difficult with evergreen trees than deciduous trees.

Competition from Tree Roots

A part of the problem with grasses growing in partially shaded areas

169

is root competition for water and nutrients. Trees should be fed by placement of fertilizer in holes 30 inches on center spaced under the area covered by the tree canopy at depths of 12 inches. This depth is below the level of grass roots. Surface roots of trees that interfere with grasses can be removed after tree fertilization since the tree will be well served by deeper roots. Grass fertilization can then be followed as on other turf areas.

Under older and larger trees, apply topdressing to maintain a relatively smooth soil surface. The great volume of tree roots, even though at some depth, will produce uplifts that are best dealt with by adding screened soil.

Renovation of Turf in Shade

Reestablishment of shade-tolerant grass should only be attempted after tree pruning and soil improvements have been made. Under deciduous trees in the cooler regions, new plantings should be planned in late summer or early fall to take full advantage of the leafless period of trees to establish the grass. Under evergreen trees in the northern regions, early spring is a better time for reseeding or sodding. In the warmer regions where warm-

Figure 14-1. Rapid preparation of seedbed, where complete renovation is needed. (Courtesy, The Toro Company)

season grass species are used, replanting should occur soon after the grass-growing season begins in spring.

It is essential that shade-tolerant grass species be used. For cooler regions, fine fescue should predominate. For warmer regions, a choice should be made between St. Augustinegrass, carpetgrass, and centipedegrass. It is often necessary to add a thin layer of screened topsoil to insure a good seedbed. Since it is difficult to prepare a seedbed 6 to 8 inches deep, reliance must be placed on treatment of the upper 2 or 3 inches of soil.

Seeding or planting may proceed in the customary manner after the seedbed is prepared. The new turf area should be kept moderately moist by watering with a fine mist-like spray until the grass is well established. Light mulching is useful in preventing soil crusting and excessive evaporation from the soil.

Fall Removal of Leaves

Under deciduous trees in autumn, leaves should be removed periodically to prevent them from covering the grass and cutting off light Care in removing leaves is essential to avoid injury to the young grass. The regular treatment of shaded turf is similar to that of other turf except that the height of cutting should be longer. In general, cutting should not be shorter

Figure 14-2. A large capacity sweeper for easy collection of leaves and trash on the turf.

than $2\frac{1}{2}$ inches. Reduced light produces a more upright growth of grasses; consequently, close mowing is more harmful on shaded grass than on turf in full sunlight.

TURF FOR SLOPING AREAS

Although healthy turf is usually established with more difficulty on steep sloping areas than on normal areas, much can be done to overcome the difficulties encountered with slopes. Successful establishment of turf on steeper slopes depends on adequate preparation of the soil before planting, the use of adapted grasses, planting at a favorable season, and precautions against washing of the newly planted area under heavy rains. The details of soil preparation and planting as described in Chapter 8 are applicable. On more difficult areas, sodding may be the most satisfactory type of planting, both in ultimate cost as well as in total effort.

Slopes Are Droughty

Slopes are characteristically droughty, since much rain and irrigation water will be lost as run-off. Cutting the grass somewhat taller on slopes than on level areas and giving special attention to adequate fertilization and liming will produce a dense sod that will lose less water by run-off than short, thin grass.

Reseeding Slopes

If a seeded turf is to be planted on steep slopes, the best season is early fall in northern regions and early spring in southern regions. Grasses that are deep rooted and drought tolerant should be used. Tall fescue should predominate, with some bluegrass in the North and bermudagrass in the South. New seedings should be protected with a covering of special erosion netting both to minimize erosion by washing and to protect against evaporation of water from the soil. These fabrics should be held permanently in place with short stakes driven in at frequent intervals. The young grass plants will grow through the open-mesh material, and the fabric may be left in place to decay and become part of the soil humus. The stakes may be removed when enough grass growth has been made to begin mowing.

Figure 14-3. A gill being used for seed bed preparation. (Courtesy, Danville Country Club)

Figure 14-4. A self-propelled dump cart. (Courtesy, South Side Country Club)

Maintenance of Sloping Turf

Somewhat greater care is needed in regular maintenance of grass on strong slopes than on normal areas. Supplemental watering will be needed more frequently, and water should be applied slowly to allow it time to penetrate without run-off. Manage sprinklers so that water is delivered at a rate equal to rate of absorption by the soil, and water until the soil is moist to a depth of 6 inches. Special attention should be given to the upper part of the slope, since this is the portion likely to suffer most severely from moisture shortages. Turf on slopes should be mowed at a longer length than normal grass, with the mower set at 3 inches or greater. However, it is undesirable to let grass grow taller than about 6 inches, since this results in a thinner turfgrass less able to retain water.

It is well to note that exposure of the slope is important; southern slopes will lose moisture faster than northern slopes and will need more careful watering. Where the slope is steep enough to cause erosion of the soil by rain or watering, a yearly topdressing with screened topsoil should be made to fill depressions that have occurred. Additional grass seed should be broadcast when topsoil is added.

RENOVATING POOR TURF

Weak thin turf that has suffered serious injuries may call for radical corrective treatment. Very often it will be possible to reestablish good turf without the necessity of going through the steps of preparing and seeding a new lawn. Improvement of the grass that is present is often feasible because healthy grass will spread and heal injuries rapidly when given an opportunity, whereas new plantings are always slow to become well established. If permanent turfgrasses occupy as much as 50 percent of the surface, the area should respond to renovation measures. These measures should be done in early fall or very early spring in northern regions and early spring in southern regions.

Diagnosis of Problems

Determine the causes of the previous turf failure. The soil should be examined as to its acidity, general condition (topsoil versus inert fill or subsoil), drainage, and compaction. The past management treatments should be reviewed, particularly of fertilization, height of cutting, and watering practices. Do not place undue emphasis on weeds, since they are symptoms of poor management rather than the cause of weak turf. Weeds may be dealt with separately, after renovation has been well advanced.

Correction

In those situations where the soil is obviously infertile and very compact, the area should be perforated to depths of about 4 inches with an aerifying machine that removes cores of soil $1/2$ to $3/4$ inch in diameter before lime and fertilizer are applied. These soil cores will be broken up in the renovation process. The tools mentioned are commonly used on parks, golf courses, and home lawns. When the surface is prepared, seeding or planting sprigs should be done with grasses adapted to the location. Stolonizing should be done by broadcasting the sprigs over the repaired area and partially covering them with topdressing. Seed should be lightly raked in. All planted areas should be watered as necessary to maintain a moderately moist soil until the new grass is well established. Mowing of the renovated areas should follow the practices recommended for new turf, despite the situations on renovated turf where established grass and new seedlings are intermingled. Watering practices also should be adjusted to meet the needs of new grass. The initial diagnosis should serve as a guide to developing a management program that can maintain quality turfgrass.

HEAVY SOILS

Droughty turf on heavy soils that crust and become very hard can be improved by an annual treatment with an aerifying machine that removes cores of $1/2$ to $3/4$ inch diameter to depths of about 4 inches. This will improve permeability of the soil to rain and watering. This treatment also will improve soil aeration and allow deeper rooting of the grass. Since the core holes permit much easier and deeper penetration of fertilizer and lime (where needed), the aerification has multiple beneficial effects. This kind of treatment greatly increases root development, and the yearly accretions of dead roots steadily improve soil structure to the depth of rooting.

WATERLOGGED SOILS IN DRY PERIODS

Some turf suffers from drought in hot, dry periods, but is damaged by waterlogging in spring and fall. This seeming paradox is the result of grass failing to develop a deep-rooting system in spring on very wet soil

Figure 14-5. Aerifying machines (top) remove cores (bottom) before lime and fertilizers are applied. (Courtesy, South Side Country Club)

because roots only occupy soil layers with reasonably good aeration. When the stress of hot, dry summer weather occurs, the shallow-rooted grass quickly succumbs to drought on such areas even though normal turf exhibits little damage. The obvious corrective treatment is to establish artificial drainage of chronically waterlogged areas by laying underground porous tile at depths necessary to carry the water to an available drainage outlet. When drainage is assured, grass production on these previously difficult areas becomes a normal process.

TREATING TRAFFIC AREAS

Unwise rolling, which compacts the soil, or heavy traffic (foot or machines) at times when the surface soil is soggy may produce enough compaction to reduce soil aeration and weaken the grass. If rolling is a cause, this practice may be corrected. If traffic is causing damage aerify the traffic areas twice each growing season. It is often helpful to mow the grass at a higher height of cut on traffic areas to provide more of a cushion to carry the traffic. Although the ultimate treatment for extreme traffic areas may be to establish a hard surface path, healthy grass will tolerate a surprising amount of traffic when given special treatment.

SODDING CRITICAL AREAS

Whenever permanent turf is needed quickly, sodding is indicated. Locally damaged areas may be quickly repaired by removal of the scarred soil and replacement with sod. However, if the turf has failed because of unfavorable soils or poor management practices, sodding may only be a temporary solution.

Before sodding, soil improvement is one of the most important prerequisites to establishing a quality lawn. After incorporation of the necessary materials, the soil should be leveled and firmed to provide a level base for the sod. The sod itself should be composed of suitable grasses for the area to be covered; that is, shade-tolerant grasses for shaded locations, drought tolerant grasses for steep slopes and soils of low water supplying power, etc. Too often, sod is selected with little regard for the kinds of grass present.

The most desirable season for laying new sod is early fall because the normal cycle of new root formation begins at that season. However, sod may be laid at almost any season with precautions to insure adequate

Figure 14-6. Cutting sod of uniform thickness for a sodding job.

moisture supply during the subsequent period of new root growth and penetration of the underlying soil.

Sod must always be kept cool, moist and well aerated after cutting to avoid damage from disease and dehydration. Lay sod on the same day it is cut. When laying sod, each piece should be firmly butted into place on ends and sides to other sods and then firmed into the soil bed by light rolling. Care in laying is very essential to producing a smooth surface. As soon as sod is laid, it should be watered moderately to stimulate new rooting and to supply enough water to sustain the turf with its severely pruned root system. Watering should continue as necessary to prevent wilting for several weeks unless rainfall is adequate.

TEMPORARY TURF

It frequently happens that there is a need for a grass cover on some areas intended for permanent turf at times when new seedings are impractical because of the season or when further disturbance of the soil (grading, traffic, etc.) is planned. To meet such needs, a very creditable green cover can be produced in about three weeks when temperatures are warm enough to permit grass growth. Perennial ryegrass may be seeded to produce such temporary turf. Seed should be broadcast at 2 to 3 pounds per 1,000 square feet and the area raked just enough to cover the seed. Watering should be provided by frequent sprinklings as needed to supplement rainfall to stimulate prompt germination and growth. Mowing may begin when grass reaches a height of about 3 inches, but these grasses must never be cut shorter than 2 inches. For southern regions in summer periods, tall fescue is probably the best choice for temporary turf in both partially shaded and sunny locations.

Figure 14-7. Verticut machines have a slicing action, but the reel on which the knives are placed rotates at a speed much faster than the forward movement of the machine. (Courtesy, Danville Country Club)

EXPLANATION OF TECHNICAL TERMS

- **Slit seeding machines** are those that cut vertical slices into the turf and drop seed in to these slits.

- **Temporary turf** is that produced by planting grasses that are not expected to live for more than a single season. Such grasses grow rapidly and, if planted thickly enough, make a rather complete green cover. Ryegrass is commonly used for this purpose.

- **Verticut machines** are those that have a slicing action, but the reel on which the knives are placed rotates at a speed much faster than the forward movement of the machine. This type of machine is very useful in removing stolons of bermudagrass where it is desired to reestablish cool-season grasses.

Chapter 15

SEASONAL SCHEDULES FOR MANAGEMENT OF TURF AREAS

GENERAL PRINCIPLES

The most effective use of materials, equipment, and labor is intimately related to the seasonal cycle of grass growth as determined by average temperatures, rainfall patterns, and length of day. The turf manager should recognize these factors when making general seasonal plans as well as in the day-to-day operations that maintain turf in a continuously usable condition and an attractive appearance, despite the heavy demands that may be made by those using the turf.

Timeliness of action is very important. Scheduling all operations to prevent the occurrence of turf weaknesses and turf damage is infinitely better than a pattern of constant alarms that try to correct unfavorable conditions after they occur. The schedules suggested are intended to be general guides. The turf manager is urged to prepare a detailed schedule too more nearly fit the particular situation. This schedule should include not only the regularly recurring maintenance and repair activities, but it should also be flexible enough to permit dealing effectively with unforeseen emergencies when these occur. Heavy storms, droughts, excessive use when soils are wet, outbreaks of pests, and crucial periods covering special activities, cannot be completely anticipated. The best turf managers not only plan ahead, but they learn by experience and do not make the same mistakes more than once.

Turf is produced to benefit people either through physical use or through its pleasing appearance. Some restraints on the use of turf by people may be required to reconcile the biological demands of the grass and its limits of endurance with the proposed use of the turf. Direct conflicts or confrontations between the turf manager and the users should be avoided. The objective is to keep the turf usable and sightly to please the users for whom it was intended. Perhaps the best starting point in preparing a schedule is

181

the winter period when there is time for taking stock and developing plans for the coming season.

SUGGESTED SCHEDULE OF TURF MANAGEMENT PRACTICES FOR THE COOLER HUMID REGIONS

Winter

- **Service and repair of equipment and machinery**—Go over all equipment and machinery needed for the growing season. Order a supply of repair parts to take care of normal replacements. This work should include any cleaning and repainting of machinery and equipment.

- **Inventory supplies needed**—Calculate the supplies required for the coming season—particularly fertilizer, lime, fungicides, insecticides, herbicides, seed, and topdressing materials. Place orders for later scheduled delivery at approximate times during the active season. Suppliers are more responsive when advanced schedules of delivery have been arranged. The turf manager cannot afford to be without important supplies when emergencies occur. If firm orders cannot be placed far in advance, suppliers should be notified of predicted needs.

- **Seasonal labor supply**—Arrange for all normal and seasonal labor. The

Figure 15-1. The latest technology in water aerification which allows use immediately after application. (Courtesy, Mollee Thomas)

best workers are always in greatest demand. Early commitments at fair wages will greatly ease the chronic labor problem. The more mechanized the operations, the greater is the need for skilled dependable workers. Be willing to employ a few untrained but promising youths. These trainees may be a salvation in emergencies; and the better ones may become permanent employees.

- **Scientific and technological advances**—Take time to become well versed in all new scientific and technological developments in the field of turf management. Also, study new developments in equipment, machinery, and improved methods of using standard items. Be particularly alert to new pests and their control, new pesticide formulations, new fertilizers, new grass cultivars, etc. Hold training sessions for the permanent crew so that they will understand the plans because there may not be adequate time for explanations during the active outdoor season.

- **Soil sampling and testing**—If not done earlier, take advantage of any period in winter when soil is not frozen to take soil samples for determination of acidity and lime requirement and current levels of soil fertility. Submit samples to a soil-testing laboratory, and request results of the analyses before spring arrives. Lime may be broadcast even in winter.

Spring

- **Winter damage repair**—Examine all turf areas to find any winter damage and carry out the corrective action needed. Note poorly drained areas, any outbreaks of snow mold, erosion damage, vandalism, and any other undesirable conditions. Move promptly to correct these conditions before other spring work becomes urgent.

- **Resodding and replanting**—Identify areas where reseeding and resodding are needed. When soil moisture will allow soil handling without danger of undue compaction, carry out all planting with adequate preparation, liming, and fertilization to meet the needs of the new grass. All such planting will to be successful if done as soon as bluegrass (as the indicator plant) begins to show signs of growth. Later planting may succeed, but early planted grass will be stronger and more capable of enduring unfavorable summer weather and foot traffic.

- **Aerifying**—On soil types that tend to become compacted easily, aerification should be done. For all soils, identify foot and vehicle traffic areas that need attention. Give them treatment with an aerifying machine as

Figure 15-2. **Pull-type aerifier in operation. (Courtesy, South Side Country
             Club)**

soon as they are dry enough to carry the machine without rutting the
soil. Aerification should precede any applications of lime, fertilizer, or
seed. It should be done early to realize full benefits from spring rains
and favorable temperatures.

- **Fertilization**—A spring application of fertilizer should be made, even
  before there are any signs of grass growth. Early fertilization will stimulate
  new top growth 7 to 10 days earlier than it would otherwise occur and
  will have equally beneficial effects on development of the new annual
  root system.

- **Rolling**—In regions where soil freezing and thawing occur in the winter,
  light rolling to firm the elevated grass crowns back into the soil should
  be done when heavy soil freezing ceases. Do this before drying winds
  cause injury, but do not roll when soil is soggy.

- **Mowing**—Adjust all mowers to the appropriate height of cut for each
  kind of turfgrass. Mowing should begin when substantial top growth has
  been made to stimulate the kind of dwarfing desired. Never cut closer
  than needed, since this will weaken the newly developing root system.
  Mow regularly when needed. Allowing grass to grow too tall and then
  cutting it back to a short length is harmful. Remove clippings on important areas whenever they are heavy enough to foster diseases.

- **Disease control**—Keep alert for diseases that occur in cooler weather and promptly treat all critical areas. In case of doubt as to the nature of the disease, take samples to the county extension agent or the state experiment station for identification and recommended treatment.

- **Watering**—In case of prolonged shortage of rain, be prepared to start supplemental watering whenever the upper 4 inches of soil appears to be dry. Water deeply, but do not repeat until soil moisture conditions indicate the need.

- **Weed control**—Apply herbicides for control of broadleaf weeds as soon as appreciable growth occurs. Make pre-emergence treatments for crabgrass and other summer weeds about the time lilacs bloom in your locality. (Lilac blooming is a seasonal indicator.)

Figure 15-3. Continue regular mowing whenever grass is long enough. (Courtesy, Mark Schroeder)

Summer

- **Mowing**—Continue regular mowing, as in spring, whenever grass is long enough to need mowing. This will produce lighter crops of clippings and may eliminate the need for collecting them.

- **Watering**—Use supplemental watering whenever the upper 4 inches of soil become dry. Install a rain gauge and keep a continuing record of local rainfall on your turfed areas. This will aid in deciding when watering is generally needed.

- **Disease control**—Be alert to the occurrence of disease, particularly in hot, humid weather. Apply control measures the same day as symptoms occur to halt damage. Use preventive treatments on areas that have a record of recurring diseases.

- **Insect control**—As warm weather begins, look for harmful insects on all turf areas that are not growing slowly. Catch the outbreaks early, with appropriate treatment, before populations build up to serious numbers. If Japanese or other beetles are numerous, treat for grubs by midsummer. For insects that harm people, such as chiggers, wasps, and ticks, apply preventive treatments at the beginning of the summer and repeat as necessary.

- **Weed control**—Use postemergence treatments for control of crabgrass and other summer annuals if preemergence treatments were not sufficient or were not applied. Such herbicides are most effective if applied when seedlings are still quite small. Treatments for broadleaf weeds may be made any time in the growing season.

Fall

- **Mowing**—Continue mowing as long as grass grows.

- **Watering**—Continue as in summer, but only as soil conditions indicate need.

- **Disease control**—Be alert for both diseases that attack in warm weather and those that occur in cooler weather.

- **Insect control**—This should be a minor problem if there was adequate treatment in summer.

- **Weed control**—Winter annual types, such as chickweed, should be controlled by treatment in early fall.

- **Fertilization**—This is a major fall activity. Apply as soon as cooler nights occur. Feeding at this stage stimulates new buds on the crowns that will develop into shoots the following year, each with its own root system. Do not skimp on fertilizer; it is poor economy.

- **Renovation**—Use aerifying machines on all compacted and impermeable areas. This should be done immediately ahead of fertilization and any reseeding. Accomplish renovation in late summer or very early fall to give grass the greatest opportunity for establishment before winter.

- **Leaf removal**—Prompt removal of leaves from deciduous trees improves usefulness and appearance of turfed areas. It is also essential for newly seeded or renovated areas to allow development of grass seedlings. Leaves cut off necessary light and foster diseases.

- **Myths**—It is not true that grass should be left uncut in fall to give winter protection. Uncut grass is a haven for over-wintering insect pests and for disease organisms. Healthy turf of adapted grasses needs no mulching to survive winters.

Figure 15-4. A backpack blower is useful in removal of undesired materials on walkways or in plantings. (Courtesy, Danville Country Club)

Turf that is in need of fertilizer, lime, improved drainage, aeration, etc., will not automatically be restored by resting over the winter. Proper corrective treatments are needed, and the sooner applied the better will be the turf.

- **Soil sampling and testing**—Each important turf area should be sampled toward the close of the growing season, and the soil samples sent to a reliable soil testing laboratory. Arrange to have recommendations made based on the reported analyses.

SUGGESTED SCHEDULE OF TURF MANAGEMENT PRACTICES FOR COOLER REGIONS WITH LIMITED RAINFALL

In general, the basic principles governing management of turfed areas are the same in these regions as for the cooler humid regions. The same grasses are used and similar seasonal temperatures prevail. There are two major differences—soil conditions and moisture supply. The soils of drier regions almost never need lime, and sometimes they are high in salt or alkali. Limited and uneven rainfall usually means a high dependence on irrigation of some effective type.

When dry land areas are first planted to grass and irrigated, the turf seems much less subject to diseases, insects, and weeds; but in subsequent years, these problems begin to appear. The reader is invited to read the preceding section for cool humid regions for the comprehensive schedule of management practices. The following outline deals primarily with features that are unique for irrigated turfed areas in dry regions.

Winter

The first five procedures are the same for these regions as for the cooler humid regions. This is a good season for carrying out all revisions of the watering system.

Spring

The first seven steps are the same for these regions as for the cooler humid regions. However, water supply is a major factor in all drier regions.

- **Watering**—The need for water will be closely related to temperatures; the higher the temperature, the greater the water consumption by grass,

Figure 14-5. City park mowing crew in Idaho. (Courtesy, Mollee Thomas)

Figure 15-6. **Winter scene of bentgrass green in Oklahoma. (Courtesy, Oklahoma State University)**

and the greater the water losses by evaporation. The turf manager not only should record all natural rainfall, but should also keep a continuous temperature record. These records must be supplemented by periodic examination of soil moisture to decide whether the grass's needs for water is being met.

- **Weed control**—Weed control is the same as for the cooler humid regions.

Summer

All management practices listed for cooler humid regions apply also to these cooler dry regions, except that irrigation continues to be the dominant requirement in drier regions.

Fall

The management practices listed for autumn in cooler humid regions are important in cooler dry regions. However, irrigation continues to be the dominant requirement. Water use will fall to a lower level as temperatures decline, but considerable water is needed as long as growth occurs. It is particularly disastrous if turfed areas go into the winter with dry soil. Killing by desiccation is entirely possible in fall and winter.

SUGGESTED SCHEDULE OF TURF MANAGEMENT PRACTICES FOR WARMER HUMID REGIONS

Winter

Except that winters are shorter in warmer regions, and there may be less time to do all the necessary things, the items to be dealt with are the same as for cooler humid regions. These are:

- Service and repair of all equipment and machinery.
- Inventory of supplies needed for the coming growing season.
- Planning for the seasonal labor supply.
- Study of scientific and technological advances.
- Soil sampling and testing.

Planning the seasonal campaign during the winter is sound management. The reader is urged to read the listing given for cooler humid regions for the winter season.

Spring

A great difference exists between the warmer and cooler regions because of the differences in grasses used. Bermuda, St. Augustine, carpet, centipede, and zoysia grasses are limited to growth in warm weather. The scheduling of all management practices must be adjusted to the temperature responses of these grasses. An additional factor is the practice sometimes followed of interplanting ryegrass as a cool-season species directly in the sod of warm-season grass in fall to give temporary green cover during winter and spring. With these adjustments, the following practices are proposed:

- **Winter damage repair**—It is desirable to make an early assessment of winter damage, and undertake repairs. Poor drainage (at the surface or in the soil), erosion damage, apparent death of sod, vandalism by misguided people, and similar matters should be corrected promptly.

- **Resodding and replanting**—This should be done when temperatures are high enough to permit growth of the grasses being used. Reseeding and sodding with warm-season grasses may be done successfully over a relatively long spring period.

- **Aerifying**—Aerifying is important for soils in warmer regions under any conditions that result in compacted, impervious surface conditions. Since

**Figure 15-7. A tractor-powered rototiller machine for quick seed bed
preparation. (Courtesy, Danville Area Community College)**

the mellowing effect of deep winter freezing and thawing is of minor
consequence in warmer regions, the use of aerifying tools becomes more
important. These treatments improve penetration of rainfall and fertilizer
and stimulate deeper grassroot systems.

• **Fertilization**—The soils of warmer regions are usually in need of substantial amounts of fertilizer. Fertilization just ahead of the normal
growing season will stimulate grass growth earlier than would otherwise
occur, and produce a denser sod. Apply fertilizer in accordance with
results of soil tests.

• **Rolling**—There is greatly reduced need for any rolling in warmer regions.
If the sod is bumpy, it is caused by factors other than lifting of grass
crowns by frost action. Treatments should be directed to actual causes.

• **Mowing**—Mowing principles are much the same for all grasses. However,
the warm-season turfgrasses are somewhat less sensitive to closer mowing
than the cooler-season turfgrasses. Mowing should begin when grasses
begin active growth to produce the dwarfing effect desired on dense sod.
Mowing heights should be as high as is compatible with use of the turf
so as to permit development of a stronger root system. Avoid mowing
neglect that produces tall growth followed by sudden close cutting, since

Figure 15-8.   Water is a major factor in successful turf maintenance.

this heavily damages sod. Remove all clippings whenever they are heavy enough to form a surface mat that fosters disease.

- **Disease control**—Warm-season grasses are susceptible to a variety of diseases, and these diseases are more virulent in sustained periods of hot humid weather. Serious outbreaks should be treated promptly. Whenever necessary, submit disease samples to the county extension agent or the state agricultural experiment station for identification of the disease and recommended treatment.

- **Watering**—The warm-season grasses differ one from another in drought tolerance, but nearly all warmer regions have periods of insufficient rainfall when supplemental watering is needed. The heavier the use of turfed areas, the greater is the need to supplement deficient rainfall in times of stress.

- **Weed control**—Apply herbicides for control of broadleaf weeds as soon as appreciable growth occurs. Make preemergence treatments for crabgrass and other summer weeds soon after the perennial turfgrass begins active growth.

Summer

- **Mowing**—Regular mowing at a suitable height should continue to keep pace with grass growth. Remove clippings when they are heavy enough to constitute a disease hazard.

- **Watering**—Use supplemental watering whenever the upper 4 inches of soil become dry. Install a rain gauge and keep a continuing record of local rainfall on your turfed areas. This will aid in deciding when watering is generally needed.

- **Disease control**—Be alert to the occurrence of diseases in hot humid weather. Apply control treatments promptly. Use preventive treatments on areas that have a record of recurring disease outbreaks.

- **Insect control**—Examine all poorly growing turf for insects. Treat all outbreaks early, before insect populations build up to serious numbers. If any types of May beetles or similar insects appear, treat the turf to kill grubs that hatch from eggs laid by the adult beetles.

  For insects that harm people, such as chiggers, wasps, and ticks, apply insecticides at the beginning of the growing season and repeat later if necessary.

- **Weed control**—Use postemergence herbicides for control of crabgrass and other summer annuals if preemergence treatments were not sufficient or were not applied. Such herbicides are most effective if applied when seedlings are still quite small. Look for infestations as soon as the turfgrass begins active growth. Treatments for broadleaf weeds may be made any time during the growing season.

- **Fertilization**—A second feeding with fertilizer should be made in mid-summer. This will sustain continued growth until cool weather arrives in fall. The amount and kind of fertilizer may be the same as for spring applications.

Fall

- **Mowing**—Continue mowing as long as grass grows.

- **Watering**—Continue as in summer, but only as soil conditions indicate need.

- **Disease control**—Be alert for both the diseases that attack in warm weather and those that occur in cooler weather.

- **Insect control**—Look for insects that escaped notice in summer. They may build up populations and cause damage in fall. Treat infestations promptly.

**Figure 15-9. Soil testing laboratory.
(Courtesy, Terra International,
Inc., Professional Products)**

- **Overseeding**—Turf managers in warmer regions have the option of overseeding permanent grass with ryegrass to give green cover through the seasons when warm-season grasses are dormant. Some soil scarification plus fertilization is needed for establishment of the ryegrass. The ryegrass should be mowed whenever its growth warrants throughout the cool seasons. Such use of ryegrass should not damage the warm-season turf-grasses.

- **Leaf removal**—This is recommended on all turf areas. Although warm-season grasses may be largely dormant when leaf fall occurs, the leaves should be removed since they tend to harbor insect pests and may foster development of cool temperature diseases. In addition, leaf cover is unsightly on turfed areas.

- **Soil sampling and testing**—Each important turf area should be sampled toward the close of the growing season, and the soil samples sent to a reliable soil testing laboratory. Arrange to have recommendations made based on reported analyses.

SUGGESTED SCHEDULE OF TURF MANAGEMENT PRACTICES FOR WARMER REGIONS WITH LIMITED RAINFALL

Winter

The paramount differences between these regions and the humid regions are the nature of the soils and the limited rainfall. Neither of these factors greatly modifies the winter schedule. For this season, the reader is invited

**Figure 15-10. Roadside erosion control tests in Oklahoma.
(Courtesy, Oklahoma State University)**

to read the more detailed discussion given for the cooler humid region, for the following matters:

• Service and repair of all equipment and machinery.

• Inventory of supplies needed for the coming growing season.

• Planning for the seasonal labor supply.

• Study of new scientific and technological advances.

• Soil sampling and testing.

In every geographic region, planning the seasonal campaign during the winter period is sound management.

Spring

Spring comes early in the warmer, drier regions. Although the turfgrasses for these regions are suitable for the humid warm regions, they may be stimulated to earlier growth because of the predominance of clear days with resulting higher daytime temperatures. The scheduling of all management practices should be adjusted to the normal growth pattern of the warmth-loving perennial turfgrasses in the locality where the turf manager is operating. The following items should receive consideration.

• **Winter damage repair**—Look for areas of poor soil drainage, soil erosion (including wind erosion), apparent death of sod, vandalism by irresponsible people, and similar matters. Identify the causes of each problem and take corrective action as early as possible.

- **Resodding, renovation and new plantings**—Whenever these treatments are needed, undertake to complete these at the very beginning of the growing season. Although soils of drier regions do not need lime, they have a great need for adequate fertility. Identity the causes of previous grass failure and take corrective action as part of the restoration process.

- **Aerifying**—Aerifying the soil may be necessary on areas that receive a great deal of foot traffic or are subjected to vehicle traffic. Accomplish this early to improve water penetration and development of a deep root system. If compaction is caused by poor internal soil drainage, install the necessary subsurface (tile) drainage at the beginning of the season.

- **Fertilization**—Nearly all soils of drier regions are very deficient in nitrogen supply. Make a very early application of fertilizer to sustain grass until the mid-season or fall application is made.

- **Mowing**—Mowing should begin as soon as active growth warrants it. Do not mow shorter than is necessary to produce the desired density and texture of sod. Regular mowing induces the kind of dwarfing needed to produce dense sod, but excessively close mowing also dwarfs the root system, which is undesirable. Avoid the bad practice of allowing taller growth and then cutting back suddenly to a short height; this damages the sod and produces an unsightly appearance.

Figure 15-11. Regular mowing at the proper height induces
the kind of dwarfing needed to produce dense
sod. (Courtesy, Danville Country Club)

- **Disease control**—Controlled watering in drier regions should greatly reduce danger of turf diseases. However, where the kind of use given the turf requires liberal watering, the manager should be alert to disease outbreaks and apply fungicides very promptly. In regions where fogs or high humidity occur (mostly at night), there is greater need for disease surveillance.

- **Watering**—This is a major factor in successful turf maintenance in warm, drier regions. Higher air temperatures cause greater use of soil moisture and greater water loss by evaporation. The objective in watering is to prevent complete exhaustion of soil water within the root zone. A desirable practice is to water sufficiently to restore soil moisture to a depth of 6 or 8 inches, but to repeat only when the soil ceases to provide enough water for grass growth. Repeated shallow watering is not wise, since it results in a shallow root system incapable of surviving the inevitable periods of moisture stress. Restore soil moisture to full root depth whenever water is applied.

- **Weed control**—Broadleaf weeds may be controlled by application of herbicides at any season. Crabgrass and other warm-season annuals may be controlled either by application of preemergence herbicides or by using postemergence chemicals. These weeds will encroach on irrigated turf, particularly those areas that are well watered. They are most easily controlled by preventive treatments or treatments applied before the seedlings develop more than two or three leaves.

Summer

All of the management practices listed for the spring season continue to be applicable during the summer. However, two treatments are particularly important at this season.

- **Watering**—Pay particular attention to watering practices. Practice deep watering to the depth of the grass-root system, but do not repeat until the soil fails to provide enough water to prevent grass wilting. Very early morning watering is preferred to evening or night watering, since the latter may encourage disease outbreaks.

- **Insect control**—Insect control is important in warm seasons. Insect activity increases as temperature rises, particularly on watered turf. Treat as soon as danger signs appear, before insect populations build up to the point that damage becomes important.

Figure 15-12. Disease, weed, and insect control are an important part of
successful turf maintenance. (Courtesy, Terra International,
Inc., Professional Products)

Fall

This is an important season, as visitors and winter residents begin to
arrive from cooler regions. With skillful management, turfed areas may be
kept vigorous and green for an extended period in these warmer regions.
Besides the regular management practices for spring and summer, there are
two matters that need special attention.

- **Fertilization**—Warm-season turfgrasses may be kept green and growing
  throughout the fall period by timely application of fertilizer. The fertilizer
  should be high in nitrogen, since this is the element most needed in
  soils of drier regions. Strong grass growth in spring and summer usually
  will have exhausted the nitrogen supplied in spring fertilization. If additional fertilizer is not given at this season, the grass will become
  prematurely dormant and brown.

- **Watering**—This continues to be an important practice for as long as
  grass remains green, even when the amount of growth is limited. Continue examining soils regularly to determine whether watering practices
  are keeping pace with grass needs. Do not waste water and labor unless
  water is actually needed by the grass. As daily temperatures fall, the
  need for water should decrease.

INDEX

A

Acid soil correction, 8, 54, 62-66, 82, 86, 97-98; *see also* Lime

Acid soils, 8, 49, 54, 57; *see also* Soil acidity

Adapted grass species, 67; *see also* Cool-season grasses; Warm-season grasses

Adult (stage of insects), defined, 145

Aeration
air circulation for turf, 149
defined, 57
machine, 47, 50-52, 104, 116
root development, 9-10, 11, 44-45, 175
sandy soil, 51
surface, 8, 183-184, 190-191, 196

Aerifying established turf, 104

Aerifying machine, 50, 52, 103, 104, 184; Figs. 5-5, 5-7, 9-3, 14-5, 15-1, 15-2

Agropyron repens, see Quackgrass

Agrostis alba, see Redtop

Agrostis canina, see Velvet bentgrass

Agrostis palustris, see Creeping bentgrass

Agrostis stolonifera, see Creeping bentgrass

Agrostis tenuis, see Colonial bentgrass

Algae, 128

Alkalinity, 62

Ammonia, *see* Fertilizers; Nitrogen

Annual bluegrass, 16, 21-23, 31, 122-123; Fig. 3-5

Annual grassy weeds 117-120

Ants, 142; *see also* Fire ants; Harvester ants

Arid and semi-arid regions, 4-5, 43, 46

Armyworms, 139

Auricles of grass, 18

Axonopus affinis, see Carpetgrass

B

Beetles, 134-137; Fig. 11-2, 11-3; *see also* Grubs

Bentgrasses, 4, 12, 15, 23-26, 30; Figs. 3-6, 3-7, 3-8; *see also* Colonial bentgrass (*Agrostis tenuis*); Cool-season grasses; Creeping bentgrass (*Agrostis palustris, Agrostis stolonifera*); Redtop (*Agrostis alba*); Velvet bentgrass (*Agrostis canina*)

Bermudagrass (*Cynodon dactylon*), 12, 15, 33-36, 42; Figs. 4-1, 4-2; *see also* Warm-season grasses
improved strain, 35-36

Billbugs, 136-137; Fig. 11-3

Blade of grass, 18

Bluegrass, 2, 19-23, 29-30; *see also* Annual bluegrass (*Poa annua*); Canada bluegrass (*Poa compressa*); Cool-season grasses; Kentucky bluegrass (*Poa pratensis*); Rough-stalked bluegrass (*Poa trivialis*)

Browning of leaf, 75

Brownpatch disease, 152-153; Figs. 12-7, 12-8

Burning of turf, 101

Buying guide, *see* Guide to buying

C

Calcium, 52-53, 54

Calibration, defined, 112

California Coast and Interior Valleys, 5, 43, 46

Canada bluegrass, 21, 30; Fig. 3-4

Carpetgrass (*Axonopus affinis*), 36, 42; Fig. 4-3; *see also* Warm-season grasses

Centipedegrass (*Eremochloa oplinoides*), 38-39, 42; Fig. 4-5; *see also* Warm-season grasses

Chemical control
turf diseases, 151-155
weeds, 116-128

Chemical herbicides, *see* Herbicides

Chemical properties, soils, 52-54

Chickweed, 125; Fig. 10-8

Chiggers, 143

Chinch bugs 137-138; Fig. 11-4

Clay, and clay loam, 44, 49, 66
drainage, 47
nutrients, 52-54

Climate
regional adaptability, 2-5
soil temperature, 51-52